ELDRIDGE CLEAVER:
ICE AND FIRE!

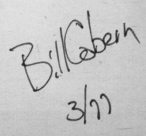

Bill Cobern
3/77

ELDRIDGE CLEAVER: ICE AND FIRE!

GEORGE OTIS

Published by
Bible Voice, Inc. P.O. Box 7491
Van Nuys, California 91409

°From "The Vanguard — A Photographic Essay on the Black Panthers" by Ruth-Marion Baruch and Pirkle Jones (Beacon Press)

This book has been prepared with neither the assistance or approval of Mr. Cleaver.

Dedicated to a Noble — the new Eldridge, child of
the King.

CONTENTS

GETTING IT TOGETHER
Preface

When Eldridge came rocketing out of exile making un-Cleaverlike waves, my antennae shot up! I couldn't believe what I was reading, and I wouldn't believe what he was saying. Still there was a subtle tone now running through his words that began vibrating with the fork of my spirit. Could it be? Eldridge Cleaver?

My curiosity was hooked. I began to collect Cleaver—both old and new. Even so I had come down with this Cleaver disease a few years behind my 23-year-old son, George, who had done a thesis on the Black Panther Party. Then the final jolt came when a friend, Pat Matrisciana, who had no knowledge of my Cleaver fascination, suddenly delivered a real, live Eldridge. It was both electrifying and confirming of a gut-feeling down inside.

Now I knew what had to be done! The controversial Cleaver was already a legend, a slice of history straining to be retold. One of the haziest enigmas of the century.

I picked up my office phone and asked YWAM for the temporary loan of young George. They graciously agreed, and he flew off to "Cleaverland", Oakland, California. There for days he mined the rich veins running all through the Bay area: newspaper files, libraries, courthouses, prisons, victims' memories, federal agents, Panther headquarters, policemen, friends and enemies.

Loaded down with tapes of Cleaver speeches, books galore, and all that Oakland loot, we disappeared in Hawaii last seen lugging a Dictaphone. Thank you, George III. Thank you, Robert Stone. And thank you, Judy Ching, for that smoking typewriter!

George Otis

THE WEEK THE WORLD SHOOK
Chapter 1

"America! America!
God shed his grace on thee,
And crown thy good with **brotherhood**
From sea to shining sea!"

Cleaver said, "We shall have our manhood. We shall have it or the earth will be leveled by our attempts to gain it!"

During that same exploding week, jailed Black Panther leader Bobby Seale shouted, "Our brother Martin Luther King exhausted the means of nonviolence with his life. . . . But unlike a panther—who doesn't attack—when we are pushed into a corner we will defend ourselves."[1] From the east coast, Stokely Carmichael railed, "Dr. King's murder signals the time for violence!"

Yes, the world was snarling: In Vietnam, Operation Pegasus pressed closer to Khé Sanh. United States warships were pounding North Vietnamese coastal positions. Huge B-52 strategic bombers and light tactical bombers were raining down their hell up north. A division spokesman said that week 116 North Vietnamese were killed, 56 Americans were dead and 401 wounded. President Lyndon Johnson's new "peace" speech was drawing angry fire from Hanoi, Peking, Moscow, Cuba and . . . Jerry Rubin.

Across the Atlantic, BOAC Captain Charles Taylor was frantically struggling with his Boeing 707 airliner which was carrying 126 people. Two minutes after takeoff, an engine had fallen off. He swung the plane in a flat left turn, attempting to reach a cross runway. On impact, the port wing fell off. The big jetliner cartwheeled along No. 5 runway and erupted in the center of Heathrow airfield. A witness said: "There was a terrific pall of black smoke and flames, with the tail still sticking up." More Americans dead.

Back in Hollywood, Gregory Peck, President of the Motion Picture Academy, announced, "The 40th Annual Academy Awards show will be postponed out of reverence."

In Europe, auto racing champion Jim Clark of Scotland was killed when he crashed in the European championship race. Clark had won the Indianapolis 500 just three years earlier.

Death seemed to be having its day.

But most shattering of all was the murder two days earlier of black civil rights hero Dr. Martin Luther King, Jr. Assassin James Earl Ray had become the object of the biggest manhunt since John Wilkes Booth.

The long-smoldering black communities erupted across the nation. One hundred fifty years of degradation, resentment, envy, bitterness, frustration were raging out of control. . . . Five thousand federal troops rolled into beleaguered, riot-ravaged Chicago where 10 people died. Widespread looting and burning broke out in Baltimore where then-Governor Spiro T. Agnew ordered 6,000 National Guard troops into the city.

Eleven-thousand-six-hundred troops tried to put a halt to the burning and looting that wrecked three areas of Washington, D.C. There were 4 deaths, 750 injuries and 3,262 arrests.

From Oakland to Chicago to Baltimore, black communities were venting uncontrollable grief and rage. In Indianapolis, Senator Bobby Kennedy sobbed, "I know how you feel. I had a brother who was murdered by a white man too." (Kennedy himself was gunned to death only a few months later on June 4, 1968, in the kitchen of the Ambassador Hotel in Los Angeles.)

For nearly 48 hours after the King shooting, moderating efforts began coming from a most unexpected source. Black Panthers took little rest during that period as they raced from one ghetto hot spot to another. On Friday, April 5, Black Panther spokesman Eldridge Cleaver rushed to an Oakland junior high school where black students were set to burn it down. They just barely responded to his forceful arguments against what he called "unfruitful, blind retaliation."

It worked marginally again and again with other angry mobs of black youth in Palo Alto, Berkeley, San Francisco, and in Richmond. The margin was just enough to prevent holocaust and death. Cleaver's strongest deterrent proved to be: "The pigs want you to riot; they're just waiting for you."[2] Cleaver was helping to keep things cool, while other cities in America were burning "from sea to shining sea."

As if these tribulations weren't enough, still another big one was gestating. A doomsday was brewing in the Black Panther flat over at 3421 Chestnut Street in Oakland.

SOW THE WIND
Chapter 2

"They sow the wind, and they reap the whirlwind."

Cleaver's immediate turf was crackling with the post-King assassination tension. Apart from that, the day, April 6, 1968, rolled along with an illusion of normalcy.

Late that morning, across the bay in San Francisco, the Black Panther de facto boss began to record notes at the *Ramparts Magazine* office, "The murder of Dr. King came surprisingly as a shock. It is hard to put words on this tape because words are no longer relevant."

By early afternoon he had his thoughts together and continued dictating, "Action is all that counts now. And maybe America will understand that. I doubt it. I think America is incapable of understanding anything relevant to human rights. I think that America has already committed suicide and we who now thrash within its dead body are also dead in part of the corpse. America is truly a disgusting burden upon this planet. And if we here in America . . . "

That's as far as he got on his article for *Ramparts.* A phone call sent him racing back across the Bay Bridge toward the Panther flat located at 3421 Chestnut Street in Oakland. The golden-eyed, handsome black grew more intense as he tooled along the Oakland street in his '61 Ford with Florida plates. Action was needed. What must he do? And what was that emergency call?

Little did he know of the myriad of forces that would orchestrate themselves over the next five hours and would catapult his own life through some of the most convoluted adventures in history.

But Cleaver had for months been contributing his own

dry sticks to a huge bonfire that was by now just waiting for one spark. . . .

Black Panther Party co-founders Huey Newton and Bobby Seale were both staring from behind prison bars and now everyone was looking to their cool, brilliant Minister of Information for leadership, and rightfully so. In the short time since Cleaver had joined the Party it had grown from a handful of Bay area radical-cats into a disciplined militant machine touching nearly every black community in America.

Cleaver's grandfathers on both his mother and father's side had been Baptist preachers. His mother, who still lives in Los Angeles, had taken her young son to a neighborhood Sunday School for a time, but his father (now deceased) left home while Cleaver was still a boy. He has been described as a railroader whose dominant characteristic was that of a hustler. It was Cleaver's father who first sowed bitter seeds of Antichrist in the youngster's mind.

Soon the boy said in effect, "No more of that Jesus ----!"

As Cleaver drove along toward the Oakland flat there was a dark elegance so characteristic of him, almost a regalness, in spite of the dark Panther "uniform." The leathery masculine scent, the shiny black leatherjacket, the light turtleneck, the black trousers, the black shoes, and the black sunglasses that shuttered his eyes, these were the Panthers' trademark—symbols of black power.

The Panthers had surfaced with a snarl over the past 18 months, invading the sacred halls of the state legislature over in Sacramento, sending a shudder of fear through the startled lawmakers. Another group of Panthers had approached a courthouse with guns. The volume of "dirty tricks" attributable to Panthers had already become legendary.

A Berkeley policeman, assigned for years to the notorious Sacramento Street and Telegraph Avenue districts, still remembers the fear generated by roaming squads "liberating" merchandise from black businessmen's stores. The loot was used to play "Robin Hood" to gain favor amongst ghetto dwellers.

Still another Oakland officer painfully recalls the blood-curdling Panther patrols. Intimidation and humiliation of the "pigs" had been one of the most visible strategies of the Party. The other visible activity was the sight of severe-clad *Black Panther* magazine hustlers sent through the community to bring about near-forced distribution.

These Panther patrols would operate with armed Party members trailing cruising police cars. Whenever the officers would stop to investigate any problem, the Panthers would pour from their own vehicle, surround, and threaten the police.

Panther hostility had also grown during the months before because they felt the police had been responding to a Sacramento and Washington secret strategy to destroy the Party. Almost every Panther leader was now in prison and those still outside were being rousted by the police on any pretext. The Panthers even took as a personal affront Assemblyman Mulford's bill to prohibit carrying loaded weapons! Bobby Seale had been arrested in Oakland for carrying a shotgun and Newton for shooting policeman Frey.

Cleaver himself was on parole and out of prison only a year and a half after serving nine "hellish" years of a 14-year sentence.

And so by Saturday evening, April 6, this longtime harassment of the police, plus the supercharged spirit of anarchy from Martin Luther King's murder, had both sides wound up to the breaking point.

The score seemed tied: Pigs 10—Panthers 10.

Yes, the "pigs" and the Panthers had each been sowing to the wind for years and now a whirlwind was just around the corner.

Something had to give. And soon it did.

When Cleaver arrived at 3421 Chestnut Street, he found not one but a score of problems awaiting him. Some had to do with "pigs," others had to do with "potatoes."

Radio stations KDIA and KSOL had been broadcasting announcements about the Huey Newton Defense Fund

Picnic scheduled for the following day, April 7, at Berkeley's DeFremery Park. Many posters had been put up and even a sound truck had been cruising through the community urging a big turnout for the Black Panther Party picnic. Preparations had to be made for a larger crowd than was originally envisioned.

Cleaver found that his friends had been busy making last minute arrangements for the Sunday picnic. The brother who owned the Soul Food Restaurant next to the Panther office at 41st and Grove was cooking the meat. Sisters were running back and forth to David Hilliard's house where the picnic supplies were being assembled.

"Cops have been following our cars," reported one Panther. "Several different cops have parked across the street with ugly pig-scowls on their faces. Now we need to go to David's for final plans."

After the way they had been hassled so long by the law, and after their leader Huey Newton had nearly been killed, they weren't taking any chances. So on the night of April 6 an armed caravan, with Cleaver driving the lead car, pulled out with the intent to go to David Hilliard's house at 34th and Magnolia.

(Author's note: The Panthers, at an earlier secret meeting place, where many weapons were kept, may have received a false report of a police ambush. Specific details are as hard to reconstruct now as identifying the cause of a fire from its smoke.)

Another grimly humorous explanation for the three-car squad bristling with weapons and ammo offered by the Panthers was that Cleaver had, in fact, "been on his way to collect some potatoes for making the potato salad" for their Sunday picnic.

But to Deputy Chief Robert Cazadd of Oakland, there wasn't a single funny thing about the Panthers. Saying, in effect, "My men have had it with their harassments—up to here!" Cazadd and a Bay area newspaper had heard a rumble that the Panthers were going to set up an ambush against the police. By this, it was reported, they attempted to set off a chain reaction with the help of Berkeley radicals and to ignite revolution all across America.

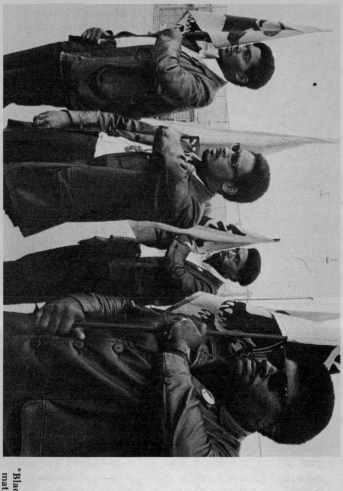

*Black Panthers in for-
mation

26

Chapter 3

•

The Panthers did certainly go out that night and many, for their own reasons, had weapons and ammo. They pulled out from the Chestnut Street flat in a four-car caravan. Cleaver was in front at the wheel of the white '61 Ford. David Hilliard, Wendell Wade and John Scott were his passengers. Immediately behind were three other Panther cars, a 1954 Ford, a Toyota and a small Austin-Healey roadster. In the trailing cars were Charles Bursey, Bobby Hutton, Donnel Lankford, Terry Cotton and Warren Wells.

The caravan headed north toward Berkeley where it stopped briefly to observe a police car, which soon sped off. After their aborted harassment of the police, the Toyota with guns in its trunk was left parked in Berkeley. The three remaining cars eased into the traffic again and cruised in the general direction of David Hilliard's house.

In Cleaver's *Post Prison Writings*, he described what happened next.

"We were only a few blocks away from David's house when, all of a sudden, I was overcome by an irresistible urge, a necessity to urinate, and so I turned off the brightly lighted street we were on, pulled to the curb, stopped the car, got out and started relieving myself.

"The two Panther cars following us pulled up behind to wait. While I was in the middle of this call of nature, a car came around the corner from the direction we had just come, and I found myself in danger of being embarrassed, I thought, by a passing car. So I cut off the flow then, and awkwardly hurried around to the other side of the car, to the sidewalk to finish what had already been started and what was most difficult to stop—I recalled I did soil my trousers somewhat.

"But this car, instead of passing, stopped and a spotlight from it was turned on and was beamed my way. Finally I could see it was the cops, two of them. They got out of the car and stood there, not leaving the car, each standing just outside."

Cleaver's conclusion was: "I had to deal with a ticklish situation and I was so close to the end I could not resist finishing. I shouted to the cops, 'Okay, okay!' I turned, trying to zip up my fly and get out in the middle of the street. Common sense told me I must have my hands up by the time I cleared the front of my car. But the cop on the passenger's side of his car started shouting and firing his gun and then the other cop started shooting. The explosions from their guns sounded like they were right in my face; so, startled, I dove for cover.

"The other Panthers started yelling and honking their horns while above my head, the windshield of my car shattered! Now there was another cop at the other end of the street shooting. In fact, shots seemed to be coming from everywhere as the block erupted with gunfire. They had us in a cross-fire so I shouted to the brothers, 'Scatter! Let's get out of here!' As I ran across the street to escape, Warren Wells was hit and let out an agonizing scream of pain as he fell to the ground."[1]

Now because Cleaver was still on parole he was personally not permitted to carry any weapon. He claims he was unarmed. Somehow he was able to successfully dodge, run and crawl to a shallow basement underneath Mrs. Nellie Pierre's ancient dwelling at 1218 28th Street. This part of Oakland is a hodgepodge of factory-type buildings sprinkled with a residue of older houses. Cleaver and little Bobby Hutton had miraculously made it alive into this one. We do know that Hutton was heavily armed.

A panting Cleaver squeezed into the darkness of that basement. His mind was spinning, his heart pounding. By now he must have felt sure the police really were trying to kill him. He didn't want to die and a kaleidoscope of thoughts played across his mind as he waited for what was yet to come.

But here is a different version of the start of that terrible 90-minute confrontation between the Panthers and the police—the viewpoint from the opposite end of the gun-barrel, so to speak. It is from the Judge and District Attorney regarding The People v. Hilliard, Docket No. 42287, signed by F.W. Vukota, Assistant District Attorney. This primarily involves the reports of Oakland police patrol car Officer Nolan Darnell and Officer Richard Jensen, who were participants in the shootout.

Under summary of offense, one portion of their report reads: "In the early afternoon hours on the 6th of April 1968, Eldridge Cleaver and David Hilliard announced there was going to be a meeting on Adeline Street near 34th Street at approximately 8:00 p.m. This was a meeting of the Black Panthers and approximately 15 Panthers showed up at the meeting. At that time Eldridge Cleaver was known as 'Section Leader' and David Hilliard was called 'Captain.' At this meeting among the 15 people attending were the individuals herein mentioned on the foregoing page.

"Guns and ammunition were issued to each of them for the purpose of patrolling the streets and killing police officers. Four cars were involved: 1961 Ford, 1951 Ford, an Austin-Healey and a Toyota. The individuals cruised around the streets of Oakland and then headed for Berkeley. While in Berkeley they observed a police officer who was standing on a corner. Hilliard drove around the block and got out of the car with the intention of crossing the block to kill the police officer. By the time they got over to where they had seen the officer, he was gone. They then returned to Oakland at approximately 9:00 p.m. that evening. After leaving the Toyota in Berkeley, they arrived at Union Street between 28th and 30th Streets and parked their cars.

"While on routine patrol in a clearly marked black and white police vehicle, Officer Nolan Darnell and Officer Richard Jensen, as passenger, proceeded south on Union Street between 28th and 30th Streets. At that time Officer Jensen observed a male Negro run from the driver's side of

29

the marked vehicle around to the passenger side and drop to the sidewalk. He also observed another Negro on the passenger side of the vehicle. Officer Jensen then observed an individual on the passenger side of the vehicle and saw him start to run in a westerly direction between the houses in that area. Officers immediately became suspicious of the possibility that the automobiles were stolen and proceeded to the immediate area. They did not in any way increase their speed, turn on the red light or make any commands whatsoever.

"After Darnell brought his vehicle to a stop and started to get out, as he did so there was gunfire from the passenger's side of the automobiles over toward the police car. This would be in an area where Officers Jensen and Darnell saw these colored individuals. Officer Jensen did not at any time fire a weapon, but sustained nine entrance wounds in his arm, back, leg and ankle. Officer Darnell fired six rounds from his .38 service revolver and wounded two suspects that were running south on Union Street. He also observed other suspects starting to run in a northerly direction on Union Street.

" 'All Hell' broke loose, whereupon the police vehicle sustained 49 bullet holes on the passenger side as well as in the window and windshield. (A second police car was burned). A Mr. Gordon Brown who was visiting his brother-in-law saw part of the shooting. He too saw individuals run on the west side of Union Street in a northerly and southerly direction. Those that did run had weapons in their hands.

"Officer Darnell immediately put out a 940B requesting help. After putting out the bulletin the police vehicles in the immediate area responded, turning on their red lights and sirens. A short time thereafter the shooting ceased and Officer Darnell heard someone say, 'Let's get out. Let's go. Let's get out of here.' "

(Author's note: To this day Kathleen Cleaver feels the shootout was a carefully arranged plot by the police to "decapitate" the Party by killing her husband. Among other things she finds it difficult to explain is how the multiplicity of police cars, 50 to 70 policemen and a SWAT van could have converged on these Party members within minutes.)

The officers' summary of offense continues: "One of the two suspects which Officer Darnell shot was Warren Wells who was . . . thereafter placed in custody at scene. Within 20 feet of Warren Wells were found a Garand rifle (30.06) caliber) and a bandolier with three clips fully loaded (each clip holding eight live rounds) which was found within six inches from where Warren Wells was laying. Also found with the gun, which was approximately 20 feet away from Wells, was an empty clip and a loaded clip with eight live rounds of ammunition. In one of the cars used by some of the defendants that were indicted were found six expended casings which had been fired from the Garand found near Wells.

"Some of the individuals that went in a northerly direction were arrested at 1267 30th Street. They were John L. Scott who had in possession at that time a 9mm automatic pistol and whose fingerprints were found inside the Austin-Healey, one of the cars involved in the offenses; and Charles Bursey who was found in one of the bedrooms with one shoe on and one off. His shoe and numerous rounds of ammunition were found in the bathroom immediately adjacent to the bedroom in which he was found. His fingerprints were also found in one of the cars at the scene. And under the house was found Wendell Wade who had in his possession at that time a 9mm pistol and numerous rounds of ammunition. Also found in the immediate area were three weapons with long barrels, rifle and shotgun type. Some were fully loaded; others had an expended round of ammunition in the chamber. Also in the immediate area where the guns were found, numerous live rounds of ammunition were picked up. Wendell Wade's fingerprint was found on a live round of ammunition that was found a short distance from the scene of the shooting.

"Those individuals that went in a southerly direction, the direction in which Warren Wells ran, left a trail of live rounds of ammunition across the Union Street in an easterly direction over toward the yard, into an outhouse where a fatigue jacket with many rounds of live ammunition was found. At the scene of the immediate shooting there were found an AR-15, 2 shotguns, 3 rifles, 6 expended rounds of ammunition, size 30.06, which were proven to have been fired by the rifle which was found near Warren Wells.

"Immediately around the corner and on 28th Street there was another shootout involving Eldridge Cleaver and Bobby Hutton in one building; David Hilliard in the other. The occupants of one house informed the Oakland Police Department there was a person hiding under their bed. This person was David Hilliard. When he first entered the apartment where this person lived the lady asked him, 'What are you doing there?' Hilliard said words to the effect that there was going to be a shooting and he would like to hide under the bed; and further if anyone asked who he was, she was to tell the person that he was her son or nephew. The other set of keys in his pocket which he took out and put on the dresser belonged to the Toyota which was found in Berkeley. Opening the trunk of the Toyota revealed numerous rifles, shotguns, and many rounds of ammunition inside the rifle. At the time of his arrest Hilliard had no shoes on."

Were police hunting Panthers that evening? Were Panthers hunting police? Or was there no hunt at all?

Black Panther Wendell Wade remembered the shootout day like this:*

"Last Saturday afternoon, April 6th, I was up at the Black Panthers headquarters at 45th and Grove. The members were discussing the picnic to be held at De-

*As outlined in People's Exhibit No. 67 (Courthouse, Oakland, California statement taken a few days after the battle April 8, 1968). Panthers subsequently repudiated their original statements.

32

Fremery Park on Sunday. I took some of the sisters shopping for food which they were going to prepare for the picnic. By the time we had finished shopping it was dark. I took the sisters home and then went over to the house on Chestnut Street. The house was located in the 3400 block of Chestnut Street. The rear of the California Hotel is right across the street from the house. The Black Panther organization pays the rent on the place; we have the bottom portion of the house and some other people live upstairs. . . .

"It was around 8:00 p.m. when I got there and there were about 10 to 15 members‘ of the Black Panthers there. When I got there all guns were just lying around on the floor of the front rooms. There were rifles, carbines, shotguns, and handguns of all types. There were also all kinds of ammunition for all those weapons there. Everyone picked out a weapon of his own choosing. I took an Astra automatic and three clips of ammunition for myself.

"After we had all armed ourselves we left and drove up around Berkeley. I was in a 1961 Ford which was driven by Cleaver. I sat in the right front seat. Bobby Hutton sat in the middle front seat. I think he had one of the military guns. It had a big wooden stock. David Hilliard was seated in the right rear seat behind me. I don't remember what kind of gun David had, but he had one kind of gun. There was another brother sitting in the left rear seat but I don't know who he was. I don't remember what kind of gun he had, but he had some kind of gun. He was about my size. He had a lot of hair, and he was real light-skinned. He looked to be about 25-27 years of age. I think he's called 'Killer.' That's all I've ever heard anyone call him.

"When we got up near Berkeley we saw two policemen up on the porch of the house. They had their black and white police car parked in front of the house. Its headlights were on and it was facing toward us. We pulled over to the side and everyone got out and went across the street and up to the corner. Before I got to the corner some of the other guys turned around and came back. We all got back into our car and went down to West Oakland. I don't know why there was no shooting at this time. I guess things were not just right. I don't think the police car had left or I would have seen it. Maybe some people came by or something. When we got back in the car everyone got back in the same seats as they were in before.

"We then drove to West Oakland and parked the car. I think we were on Poplar Street but it may have been Magnolia. It was near 28th Street anyway. We were parked in front, in the 1961 Ford, directly behind us was parked the 1954 Ford; I think that car belongs to Charlie Clayborne. I think he was driving but I'm not sure. Charles Bursey and John Scott were in the car also. There were two or three guys in the old Ford also, but I don't remember who they were. All these guys had guns too. . . .

"Behind the old Ford was a kind of orange colored sports car. I think Robert was driving it. I think there was only one other person in this car, but I don't know who it was. They were armed too, but I don't remember what kinds of guns they had.

"We left the Toyota up in Berkeley and the guys who were in it got into Clayborne's Ford. I don't remember who had been in the Toyota . . . these guys all had guns too.

"After we had parked our cars . . . we all started getting out of our cars when that police car pulled up. Everyone just started running and hiding. The police car just stood there for about a minute shining its spotlight around. Then the shooting started. I was hiding in the grass in the driveway of a house on the same side of the street we were parked on. As far as I can remember all of us were out of our cars and hiding before any shooting started. . . . There was gunfire coming from both sides and I ran and jumped over a fence and through a backyard. I fell on top of a shotgun. I picked it up and ran into Scott and Bursey. We all jumped over another fence. I don't know who dropped the shotgun that I fell on. We then jumped on the roof of another garage and then down into another backyard. Some kids opened their back door and three of us ran into the

34

house. And I could see the police out in front so I turned around and ran back outside and hid under the house. I remained under there until the police found me. I left the shotgun lying out in the yard.... I don't know exactly what we all were going to do that night. All I know was that we were going out to do some shooting. This is a true statement given freely and voluntarily without threat or promises."[1]

Signed by Wendell Wade and later repudiated.

This is the way Black Panther Terry Cotton saw it:*

"On the 6th of April about 4:00 p.m. I walked over to 1478 Adeline, I think near 34th Street. I was told there was going to be a meeting of the Black Panthers at 8:00 p.m. I just waited around 'til 8:00 p.m. About 15 people showed up at 8:00. Eldridge and David, Section Leader and Captain, said, 'Let's go out and patrol the area and see what the cops are doing in the area.' We all got different guns. I got a .30 caliber carbine. Eldridge had to show me how to load the gun.

"Eldridge Cleaver who was taking Bobby Seale's place while he was gone said, 'Let's go out and scout around and if the cops stop us we'll have a shootout with them.' We all took our guns and got in four cars.... A little guy named Bobby and another guy who is a leader of the Black Panthers in San Francisco got in the white car with Cleaver...."[2]

We have heard from participants on both sides. Now, let us take a look at the newspaper accounts. The press always strives to present facts but no reporters were there, so they too had to depend on witnesses and "second-hand" reports.

On the morning following the shootout, one Bay area newspaper covered the shootout as follows:

"Saturday night's raging 90-minute gun battle between nine armed men and police in West Oakland left one dead and four wounded.

*Also part of People's Exhibit No. 67, Courthouse, Oakland, April 8, 1968, and subsequently repudiated.

35

"The wounded included two police officers, hit by shotgun blasts, and two suspects, Eldridge Cleaver, 32, Minister of Information for the black militant group, and Warren Wells, 21.

"Nine suspects, including Cleaver and Wells, were held on a variety of felony charges ranging from carrying a concealed weapon to attempted murder.

"All suspects are Negroes. Police said all are members of the Black Panther Party.

"Police seized an arsenal of weapons and ammunition. Some of the 18 rifles and handguns seized were military type, not obtainable on the open market.

"Police said that Hutton and Cleaver were holed up at 1218 28th Street and were armed with 9mm automatic pistols, 2 AR-15 and M-14 military automatic rifles and a large supply of ammunition, some of it armor-piercing. . . .

"Wells was hit in the buttocks with a police slug and was taken to Highland Hospital under guard.

"Cleaver, a staff writer for *Ramparts Magazine*, was shot in the leg, apparently during the battle. . . .

"Oakland patrolmen Richard Jensen and Nolan Darnell were hit by shotgun blasts earlier. Jensen, the more seriously wounded, was reported in fair condition. Darnell said he got off three shots, one of which hit Wells. Jensen, seriously wounded, did not fire his gun.

"Two other officers suffered minor injuries. . . .

"Oakland Deputy Police Chief Cazadd said the Saturday shooting started with what he called a 'planned ambush' of police. He said that at 9:09 Saturday Jensen and Darnell stopped their patrol car in the 2800 block of Union Street to check a man they said was crouching down behind an auto with Florida plates. The officers were getting out of their car when they were caught between a cross-fire from both sides of the street and in the rear. Their car was blasted with 49 bullet holes. Another police car was burned.

"Officers radioed for help. Four dozen officers, some

from Emeryville Police Department, responded. A two-block area was sealed off."[3]

So much for our search for answers to the questions: "Who?" and "Why?"

Meanwhile let's go back to that 28th Street basement where little Bobby Hutton and Eldridge Cleaver were fighting for their lives.

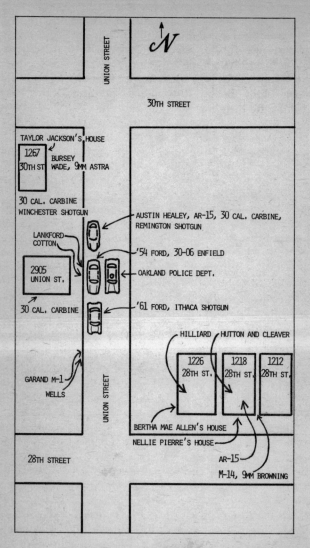

Site of Police-Panther shooting, April 6, 1968

Shoot-out neighborhood today

REQUIEM FOR LITTLE BOBBY
Chapter 4

"Wherever death may surprise us it will be welcomed,
provided that this, our battle cry, reach some
receptive ear; that another hand reach out to pick up
the gun, that other fighting men come forward to
intone our funeral dirge to the staccato of machine
gun fire and new cries of battle and victory."

—Che Guevara

Maybe 15 black and white police cars, a SWAT van, a
couple of fire engines, 75-100 police and firemen, 1,000
rounds of fire and a half-dozen blasts of tear gas: All
this—just for little Bobby Hutton and the Big Man, Cleaver.

This unlikely twosome huddled and screamed in that
creepy basement fighting for their lives. Cleaver, the
golden-eyed giant of a man of the brilliant mind, and the
little man-child with the lethal smile.

Bob Avakian, a reporter for *Ramparts,* once wrote, "Hutton took himself very seriously and demanded respect as a
man. . . . He proved to be one of the toughest, guttiest,
most disciplined and serious of all the Panthers. Yet there
was a certain quality about little Bobby, a kind of twinkle
in his whole personality . . . he was a black liberation
soldier . . . and he had an infectious smile that made you
feel there must be something basically very good about
everything he was into."[1]

Hutton's attorney, Malcolm Burnstein, added, "He was a
bright, joking kid—not snarling or hostile. He didn't believe
in nonviolence of the Martin Luther King type, but he
believed in violence only as a defense of the black people."

His mother told of times Bobby would come home at
night. How they would read the papers together and talk

over all of the day's happenings. In the weeks before Bobby's death, he was reading the heavily communist-slanted writings of W.E.B. DuBois.

Bobby Seale, co-founder of the Party, saw Bobby Hutton a few years earlier when he first came into the Oakland Poverty Center on a Saturday afternoon. The boy was constantly in trouble at school and now he was looking for a job at the Center. The day's work had been finished and most of the boys hunkered down to do a little low-stakes gambling.

Seale recalls his first conversation with the youngster who, uninvited, sat right down to play. Seale said to Bobby and the cluster of gamblers, "Well, you cats can't gamble without me. So let's get it on down there. Now what are you gambling for anyway?"

Bobby Hutton piped up, "You don't need to be gambling because the whole operation is always against you."

Seale laughed, "Oh, man, you don't know what you're talking about, baby! You're just one of those jive squares, Bobby!"

All of them knew Bobby was lying about his age. Hutton said he was 16 so he could get into the Poverty Center jobs; but his face said he was a young 13. Bobby was a lot older in his head; he had already survived more crises and experiences than most 60-year-old whites.

Newton, the other Panther co-founder, also took a liking to little Bobby Hutton immediately. Seale has described the early days when the Panthers were an unorganized gang of blacks with Huey Newton as the prime, though unofficial, force. The gang just floated around getting their kicks from ripping-off, womanizing, drinking, talking revolution and Marxism, harassing the police, sleeping and gambling.

But Huey Newton, somehow, had a gift for understanding the fundamentals of crime and constitutional law. For a short time Newton attended a night class on criminal law at a nearby college. His professor found him at the top of the class. He became a genius at twisting the law to the benefit of his revolution. And he was also a miracle worker at harnessing talent like that of little Bobby Hutton.

One day Huey told Seale and little Bobby it was time to give structure, organization and substance and build their gang into a movement. And so in a few days, little Bobby Hutton, Huey Newton and Bobby Seale pooled their Poverty Center money to pay the first $150 month's rent on the 56th and Grove "headquarters." These three painted a sign and hung it proudly in the window. It read, "BLACK PANTHER PARTY FOR SELF-DEFENSE." It was January 1, 1967.

Some people laughed. But behind their sign grew something that was far from a laughing matter. It was to grow with money, guns and guts.

And their mutual hatred for "pigs" wasn't all that bound them together. There was another reason, a smoldering dream in each of the hearts of this pioneering threesome: the dream of a Communist sitting in each governor's chair; elimination of the office of the President; and a Central Committee carrying forth in our Senate chambers.

One day, some of the "brothers" were parked outside an Oakland doctor's office waiting for Huey to come out. One of them spotted a fascinating article in the newspaper. It was the first news about the role Mao's little *Red Book* was playing in the Cultural Revolution that was shaking up China at the moment. The Panthers showed the piece to Huey when he got into the car and he read it with glee.

Then Huey said, "You know what? I know how we can make some money to buy us some guns. There are 26,000 students over at Cal and all those leftist radicals in Berkeley. They'll buy the *Red Book*."[3]

They drove over to the China Book Store in San Francisco and, as a test, bought up two batches of the *Red Book* for 30¢ apiece. They went like hotcakes on the Cal campus at one dollar. Little Bobby Hutton drove back to Frisco and cleaned out the entire China Book Store's supply of Mao's *Red Book*. Their sale raised enough to buy a few guns and now they were in business.

As Treasurer of the Panther Party, Bobby Hutton became proficient with the tools of his office—guns. Some say he was " gun happy."

The Great Book says, "Those who live by the sword will die by the sword." But little Bobby Hutton was reading a different book and marching to a different drummer. Let's move to the dark stage of Bobby's final scene.

Is that a dirge I hear?

°Little Bobby in Panther window shattered by Police bullets

PIRKLE JONES

MIRACLE ON 28th STREET
Chapter 5

The time was 9:26 p.m. Twenty-two minutes had elapsed since police car 1729, manned by Oakland police officers Nolan Darnell and Richard Jensen, had its windshield blown out. Within minutes it was perforated with 49 more bullet holes and soon a second black and white was burning furiously.

Officer Darnell was hit in one shoulder. His partner, Jensen, took nine gunshot wounds in his back, arms and leg. In spite of his pain, Darnell managed to grab the police radio microphone and called, "Attention all units, we have a 940B! Officers need help!—2900 block of Union." Within 15 minutes Panthers Donnel Lankford and Terry Cotton were handcuffed by the police on the sidewalk where the shooting first broke out.

Panther Warren Wells was shot during the first volleys while fleeing from the scene and was finally captured by Officer Hooper and Inspector Heaton hiding in some nearby bushes.

A few minutes later Panthers John Scott, Charles Bursey and Wendell Wade were apprehended along with their weapons at the Taylor Jackson residence, 1267 30th Street. Officers Lewis, Nelson and Tarabochia nabbed the trio.

The seventh of the nine Panthers, David Hilliard, was captured while hiding under Bertha Mae Allen's bed at 1226 28th Street, by Officer Newton.

That left only Bobby Hutton and Cleaver unaccounted for.

By now it was 9:26 p.m. and the scene around Mrs. Nellie Pierre's house at 1218 28th took on the sights and sounds of a B-grade gangster movie, sirens screaming in the distance, the crackle of gunfire, splintering of wood and glass, and the shrill oaths of keyed-up men. Dogs growled, barked and howled, adding their eerie contribution.

The set was lighted by a dozen police cars, making strange patterns in the gunsmoke as it drifted up through the night air. As they finished the job of capturing the other gunmen, more and more police were taking their places around this final Panther fortress.

The apparently unarmed Cleaver and heavily armed Bobby Hutton had crawled away from the three Panther cars, then jumped up and sprinted across Union Street after the shootout first erupted. Now they zig-zagged between houses and scampered over fences through a rain of bullets.

Suddenly they found themselves trapped in the open, on top of a small shed behind 1218 28th. Hutton shouldered his rifle, whirled and began to squeeze-off rounds in all directions. The pursuing cops scampered for cover, giving the two fugitives time to break into the junk-filled basement.

Little Bobby Hutton had, true to his gun-loving nature, brought along a couple of big weapons and plenty of shells. The basement was not "exactly" a fortress, but they were thankful for what little protection the walls of Nellie Pierre's ancient dwelling offered. The police rounds began to accelerate to eight or ten a minute . . . most of them penetrating those walls as if they were paper.

Some years later Cleaver was asked what it felt like to be trapped down there with police bullets coming from all sides. He said, "It was like being the Indians in all the cowboy movies I had ever seen."

Hutton and Cleaver lay pinned to the floor, protected only by an 18-inch-high cement foundation, while bullets whined and ricocheted above and around them.

During a brief lull in the firing, both men scrambled to build a barricade from anything they could get their hands on. As Cleaver momentarily stood to grab a box, he was sent spinning and crashing to the floor, hit in the chest by a tear-gas canister fired through the basement window.

As the cellar began filling with biting, acrid gas, the

48

shooting again broke out at a still more frantic level. Both of the blacks were now coughing as their lungs began to burn. Both suffered a blinding, searing pain in their eyes. Then a police bullet exploded against Cleaver's leg.

The ever-loyal little Bobby Hutton dropped his guns and commenced to strip the clothes from his big wounded friend. Little Bobby felt in the darkness to see how badly Cleaver was hit. Had he asked, Cleaver would have said, "Forget me. Take care of yourself"; for, half delirious with pain, Cleaver was saying good-bye to his life.

Somehow the image of Kathleen danced before him and his drifting thoughts recalled crowds of milling enthusiastic people he had spoken to as a candidate for President on the Peace and Freedom Party ticket. But suddenly the applause he was "hearing" turned into the roar of battle as he heard little Bobby cry out, "What are we going to do?"

More tear-gas canisters were now being lobbed in: and right on target. One started a fire. They both knew it was over. Bullets, tear gas, smoke—and now the fire had finally withered their stubborn wills.

Little Bobby helped the semi-naked Cleaver to his feet. They began to yell out together to the police. "Stop shooting, we're coming out!" They staggered through the basement door together. Their swollen, blinded eyes were struck by the glare of police searchlights. Cleaver's shot-up leg buckled under him. They both fell into an exhausted heap. Two police officers rushed in.

As they all struggled back up, little Bobby Hutton, for reasons unknown, sprang from a half-crouch darting toward an opening in the ranks.

Someone yelled, "He's got a gun!"

Another shouted, "He's getting away!"

Two days later Cleaver told reporters, "The pigs pointed to a squad car parked in the middle of the street and told us to run to it. I told them I couldn't run. Then they snatched little Bobby and shoved him forward telling him to run to the car."[1]

Cleaver, right or wrong, believed the police wanted them

49

to make a run for it to justify killing them both. But Cleaver could no longer run.

At any rate, little Bobby Hutton hadn't sprinted 20 feet before his body looked like a rag doll being spun and shaken by some giant, invisible hand as seven bullets crashed into his thin frame.

From the author's studies of volumes of police, newspaper and court records, there appears to be no hard evidence to prove Cleaver fired a gun at any time during that fateful evening. As a matter of fact, only two policemen, Officers Schlim and Coffman, ever identified Cleaver, and then not until he emerged from that basement.

The attorney for the defendants, in his motion to dismiss the indictment, said, "While it is apparent from the testimony of several witnesses that defendant (Cleaver) emerged from the basement of 1218 28th, and while it is apparent from the testimony of several witnesses that defendant (Cleaver) had been in that basement for an extended period of time, there is no evidence as to what he did while there, including no evidence that he fired a weapon, or that he had possession of a weapon. . . . Cleaver was not alone in the basement; Bobby Hutton, who was soon after killed by the police just outside the basement, was also in that basement for the same period of time . . . and since there was no evidence to indicate that defendant (Cleaver) fired any weapons, i.e., evidence that Hutton did not fire all shots. . . ."[2]

Equally important was Cleaver's own burning conviction that these same police had maneuvered this night to once-and-for-all kill him personally and the Party. If this were true, his legal fate may not rest on proving whether he ever did any shooting that night.

Still, there was a miracle on 28th Street!

Few men have ever survived through 90 minutes of such fury. It was as though God had other plans for Cleaver that Cleaver himself didn't know. Had angels been dispatched to protect the life of a rebellious black so that one day he might have another chance?

All miracles are bizarre, for by definition they must defy natural laws and explanations. As he left that smoking scene alive, Cleaver himself was a miracle. Even with eyes swollen shut, wounded in the chest, shot in the leg and broken-hearted, he didn't consider his survival any miracle right then.

The revelation of this miracle would come slowly; not until Cleaver's eyes were fully opened.

But weep for little Bobby, there were no miracles for him.

°Cleaver and Hutton's basement shoot-out hideaway. The spot where Bobby Hutton was killed.

CAST OF CHARACTERS
Chapter 6

OTHER BLACK PANTHERS—PAST AND PRESENT

HUEY NEWTON: Co-founder of Black Panther Party and its Minister of Defense. Injured in gun battle, and charged with killing Oakland police officer, John Frey. Now a fugitive from prosecution living in Havana. Newton is still directing the Panthers from Cuba through Elaine Brown, the Party's current Chairperson. (Newton was in jail on the night of the shootout.) See photo.

BOBBY SEALE: Co-founder of Black Panther Party and its Chairman. Author of the book, *Seize the Time*. Was charged in Connecticut for murder, conspiracy and kidnapping. Vanished under mysterious circumstances and some would not be surprised if Seale has been killed by the radicals. (Bobby Seale was also in jail on the night of the shootout.) See photo.

BOBBY HUTTON: Very first member of the Black Panther Party and held office of Treasurer. Smiling, baby-faced, fierce. Killed as he and Cleaver emerged from the besieged Oakland dwelling. Hutton was also involved in the initial firing on police and later very heavily involved in shooting from the cellar hideout. The Party's martyr symbol, affectionately called "li'l Bobby" or "Baby Bobby." (He was 17 on night of the shootout). See photo.

DAVID HILLIARD: Panther Chief of Staff or National Captain. Was riding in Panther lead car with Cleaver at time the firing opened up on Union Street. Caught unhurt, by police, next door to the shootout hiding under Bertha

Allen's bed. Hilliard has been charged with attempted murder. Later charged in federal courts with threatening to kill President Nixon. Rumored now to be working as a long-shoreman. (He was 25 on night of shootout.)

JOHN SCOTT: Was also riding with Cleaver in lead car. Arrested after gun battle by Officers Lewis, Nelson and Tarabochia. Was armed with Astra automatic 9mm pistol when discovered hiding in the Taylor Jackson dwelling, 1267 39th Street.

CHARLES BURSEY: Captured in crawl-space under the Jackson home with another 9mm Astra automatic pistol lying nearby. Captured by same police team. (He was 21 at this time.)

WENDELL WADE: Also captured at Jackson home by Officers Lewis, Nelson and Tarabochia of the Oakland police force. (He was 23 at time of shootout.)

DONNEL LANKFORD: Was riding in middle car of the three-car Panther caravan. Captured and cuffed outside 1954 Ford by Sergeant Hooper on Union Street. Found carrying a black sock full of shotgun shells and other ammunition. (He was 18 at time of shootout.)

TERRY COTTON: Captured by Sergeant Hooper with Lankford, and also carrying a supply of ammunition. Cotton was yelling, "Don't shoot! We didn't have anything to do with the shooting." (He was 21 at time of shootout.)

WARREN W. WELLS: Called "Killer," captured by Officer Hooper and Inspector Heaton hiding in nearby bushes. He had been shot while running to escape. Found with a bandolier of M-1 ammunition. Both a Garand rifle and an army M-1 lay nearby.

KATHLEEN CLEAVER: Former Communication Secretary of the Party. Responsible for Party newspaper, *The Black Panther*, along with her husband, the Minister of Information. In 1968 Kathleen ran for 18th Assembly District seat in San Francisco. Mother of the two Cleaver children, son Maceo, 7, and daughter Joju, 6. (Not involved with shootout.) See photo.

ELAINE BROWN: Current Chairperson of the Black Panther Party. Described by Huey Newton as "Comrade Elaine Brown." (Not involved with shootout.)

MISCELLANEOUS CHARACTERS

JERRY RUBIN: Former sports reporter. Author of the zany but potent revolutionary book, *Do It!* Outside agitator who claimed he was trying to destroy the university at Berkeley. Ran for mayor of Berkeley and also for Vice-President of the United States during Cleaver campaign. Project Director of "March on the Pentagon." Rubin, along with revolutionary Abbie Hoffman, created the Yippie movement. In Chicago during 1968 they mobilized the notorious demonstrations during the Democratic National Convention. As a derogatory gesture, Rubin liked to spell the U.S.A.'s other name, "Amerika." (Not involved with shootout.)

JUDGE RAYMOND SHERWIN: Solano County Judge who some weeks after the shootout ordered Cleaver released from Vacaville Prison, on the grounds he had been jailed for political reasons. Sherwin's ruling to free Cleaver later overturned by a higher court, but too late.

BAY AREA POLICE

CHARLES GAINES: Oakland Police Chief in 1967 at 34 years of age. In the months following shootout Chief Gain issued orders forbidding his police to fire guns for any reason whatsoever excepting in self-defense. Even if police saw a crime taking place and could not get criminal to stop, firing of weapon was forbidden. On January 12, 1976, Gaines became San Francisco's Chief of Police.

ROBERT CAZADD: Oakland Deputy Police Chief who stated his position to newspapers that the shootout was a result of a Black Panther's "planned ambush." (It is rumored that other Bay area police were operating as an unofficial vigilante squad to neutralize the Panther Party. It is certain that the Panther headquarters was shot up. See photo, headquarters.)

NOLAN DARNELL: Oakland policeman riding in first black and white patrol car to spot the Panther three-car caravan. Fired three rounds from his .38 service revolver. Radioed first "940B" for more police help.

RICHARD JENSEN: Oakland policeman riding in patrol car with Officer Darnell on night of shootout. Shot nine times during time of initial firing on Union Street. Never got off a single return shot.

OFFICER HOOPER: Captured Warren Wells lying in bushes near shootout area.

INSPECTOR HEATON: Assisted in capture of Wells.

OFFICER LEWIS: Helped in capture of Panthers Scott, Bursey and Wade at the Jackson residence, 1267 30th, near shootout.

OFFICER NELSON: Assisted in Scott, Bursey and Wade capture along with Officers Lewis and Tarabochia.

OFFICER TARABOCHIA: Assisted in Scott, Bursey and Wade capture along with Officers Lewis and Nelson.

OFFICER SCHLIM: Among policemen ringing Nellie

Pierre's basement at 1218 28th where Cleaver and Hutton were trapped. Schlim identified Cleaver at time of surrender when he emerged from basement door.

OFFICER COFFMAN: Also among policemen ringing final shootout at Pierre basement. Along with Officer Schlim, helped identify Cleaver at the end of gun battle.

OFFICER OTTO: Fired tear-gas canisters into basement hideout.

These were among the 70 to 100 law enforcement and fire department personnel marshalled at the shootout scene.

°Bobby Seale, Chairman and co-founder of the Black Panther Party.

PIRKLE JONES

°Huey Newton, co-founder of the Black Panther Party.

RUTH-MARION BARUCH

REFLECTIONS OF A BERKELEY COP
Chapter 7

It is simply impossible to gain a clear and comprehensive perspective on the Panther situation unless it is viewed from more than one vantage point. A recent interview with a Berkeley policeman employed in the Bay area law enforcement during the volatile '60s provides some fresh and intriguing glimpses.

QUESTION: Could you give us a little background on some of the things you were doing in your work with the police department?

POLICEMAN: I started with the City of Berkeley as a policeman in 1963. At that time Mario Savio was just starting with the "Free Speech" movement. Berkeley was pretty wrapped up in the university's problems. I worked on patrol in Berkeley as a beat officer for several years and then in what we called the Suppression Unit detail for a couple more years.

We did a lot of shoplift work, burglary stake-outs, narcotics, and prostitution. From there I went back to patrol and then I was asked to work the Telegraph Avenue area as a uniformed beat patrolman—not so much in the area of suppression as it was in the area of trying to relate to the "heads" or the street people. To be a go-between bridging the cops and the hip people.

At that time I had almost as much trouble with some of my peers in the department, but not physical trouble. A few in the police department felt like, "Here we are trying to enforce the law, and there I was smiling and getting along with the street people." Some didn't go for that at all. It was a difficult position for me, but a challenging one.

At one stage, while I was a foot patrolman on Telegraph, we had a black officer named J.J. Gwen, who was working a foot beat on Sacramento Street. The captain in charge of the whole program decided, just to help the racial thing, he would switch us and put J.J. on Telegraph and put me on Sacramento Street. Sacramento was a very rough area—lots of gambling, narcotics and a lot of very militant black people. J.J. told the department it wouldn't work. He said I wouldn't stay alive for more than a couple of weeks, if I stayed alive that long. And I told them that I didn't think it would work either. Not because of me and my approach to people, but simply because I was white.

But they wouldn't listen to either me or J.J. Anyway J.J. was supposed to take me down there and introduce me to some of the merchants. I felt, "Well if something's going to happen, it's going to happen. I've entrusted my life to God and that was just it." Anyway J.J. and I went down there and he introduced me to some of the merchants and they were just appalled at the thought that the department was going to send me down there.

A number said in so many words, "If the captain wants a white man down here tell him to come down here and walk the streets himself and see how long *he* lasts." The merchants didn't want me there because they feared for my safety, and it would be bad for them if a white cop got killed down there. Finally the department changed its mind about sending me into that very dangerous assignment.

My whole goal as a walking beat patrolman on Telegraph Avenue was to try and develop some kind of rapport between at least one cop and the people on the street. I think it finally worked out fairly well. From there I spent another year on patrol and then later was assigned as a horseback patrolman in the regional parks. For the past year I've been flying a helicopter for the regional parks.

QUESTION: Did you ever see the Black Panthers cruising when you were working the Telegraph Avenue area during the late '60s?

POLICEMAN: Definitely. They were very obvious in their presence; also while selling their newspaper on the streets. The in-thing at that time for the guys who were members of the Party, was dark clothes and a black leatherjacket. That was what I had as an idea of what the Panthers' normal dress was. That was confirmed by the fact that a lot of the young fellows who were selling the Panthers' scandal sheet were dressed in that manner.

QUESTION: Would you say there existed at that time a fear within the minds of police because of the Black Panthers' militancy?

POLICEMAN: I would say so—definitely, because they (Panthers) would make no bones about the way they felt. That is to say, they would shoot a cop. They wouldn't hesitate to use weapons. They had weapons within their headquarters—I believe it was on Grove. We had good information that there was a large stockpile of weapons and explosives in that headquarters. And there certainly was a fear or awareness of the fact that these men hated white people, particularly white policemen, and would, if given the opportunity, kill a cop or a white man. So definitely, there was fear and apprehension about members of that Party.

QUESTION: Did you see the Black Panthers as a group of people who were excited and influenced by eloquent leaders like Huey Newton, Cleaver and people like that; or did you feel that as individuals they knew what they were doing?

POLICEMAN: If I were to go to one of those sides which you have just mentioned, I would say they were largely made up of men who were hostile anyway and then were brought into some semblance of order by the leadership they had. I feel they were men who on their own were very much capable of the acts they were talking about doing.

QUESTION: Do you think that the leadership of the Party through their Marxist-Leninist ideology would see themselves as protecting the black community against the invading white forces? That, perhaps, this gave the Panthers justification for doing other things they really would like to do anyway?

POLICEMAN: I feel that is very true, and I feel very strongly about that—that Panthers were not supported that much by the black community. The black community saw a lot of what their young men were doing and didn't like it, and wanted no part of it. Many wanted it to be suppressed. I knew of numerous occasions when Panthers would go in and commandeer foodstuffs from black-owned stores. Then they would go and present it to schools as some great gesture of their benevolence. And yet they were stealing from someone else to give out these things—to get the cameras on them.

QUESTION: It seems like the Panthers often tried to make things look political. When they were arrested they were "political prisoners." Their literature indicates they felt the police were really after their leadership. If the police could jail their leadership, Seale, Newton, Cleaver, Hilliard, etc., they could then force the Party to disintegrate. Were the police thinking of going after the leaders to decapitate the Party?

POLICEMAN: I honestly don't believe so. The main concern of the police, as I saw it, was the threat of violence and the crime that was occurring as a result of the group. They were concerned about controlling what these young men were doing, more than going after them as a political body.

QUESTION: There have been some interesting revelations lately. A lot of the radicals were incensed when they heard that the FBI had made a point of really zeroing in on some of these organizations like the Panthers. They felt singled out for a certain amount of harassment. What do you think about this?

POLICEMAN: Again, I feel very strongly about our society having the ability and freedom to attempt to control, or at least educate the citizenry with regard to organizations that are attempting to tear our society apart. The more controls we put on the FBI and other such agencies, the more chance these radical organizations (such as the Panther Party, the Weathermen and the SDS) will have at going ahead with their violent plans to overthrow our government. I can't speak for the FBI, but there's not a doubt in my mind that they were trying to infiltrate, and educate themselves with regards to the Panther Party. If you call this harassment, then I think the harassment was well justified and needed at that time.

QUESTION: What about the allegation that they were trying to set different factions within the black community against themselves so that they would eliminate one another?

POLICEMAN: I don't know whether they attempted to do that or not. I think that an organization which is attempting to overthrow our government is morally wrong. I would decide that any proper tactics I could use that were not morally wrong to attempt to break down what they were doing ... would be all right. There was a lot of infighting within their organization and that may have been set up by some outside agency. I don't know.

QUESTION: Moving to the time of the shootout. Two days prior to that there was the assassination of Dr. King and all over the country there were riots erupting. What kind of instructions were you given in dealing with possible problems in the Oakland area?

POLICEMAN: I don't really recall being given special instructions. Everyone was uptight, but we weren't given special instructions. We were constantly reminded of what was going on and to be extremely careful and alert toward any kind of trouble.

QUESTION: What were some of your own feelings and maybe some of the fellows that you worked with? It is alleged that at that time a lot of policemen were trigger-happy. Some claimed that was one of the reasons the shootout took place with the Panthers.

POLICEMAN: I don't think that's true. I wouldn't say the police were trigger-happy at that time. I can remember, I don't know if this was in '68 or not, but there was a flyer circulated all over Berkeley. It gave specific instructions on how to disarm and kill a policeman. I was walking the Telegraph Avenue beat at that time and so for a while I carried an unloaded holster gun and a loaded pistol in my pocket. I'm sure other policemen did various things as a result of this flyer. I did that without the express permission of any commander. I just decided that because this flyer had been out, because this was on the mind of at least a certain type of person, that it might just put enough of a seed into their mind. They might decide it was worth a try. So I took this precaution. Shortly thereafter I returned to carrying a loaded holster weapon. But then I had my gun taken away from me by a suspect on the street. Fortunately, I wasn't shot with my own gun, but it was a very frightening situation.

QUESTION: It's been alleged that maybe the police in the 1968 shootout "set up" the Panthers. What is your opinion? Knowing police work, the extra men, equipment, special weapons needed to set up an operation like that shootout, is it likely? Is it possible that it was a setup by the police to get the Panthers?

POLICEMAN: I really don't think so. I know that in Berkeley when a firefight like this occurred there were certain cars sometimes driven by sergeants or by specific individuals which were set up with special equipment and weapons just for this kind of a situation. So I don't necessarily think this would have to be a setup because the City of Oakland experiences more of this kind of situation than Berkeley. There's a larger population; the police are better equipped to handle that kind of situation than Berkeley. I don't think it would be necessary to have a planned setup situation with special equipment and weapons. That's just my opinion. That's not to say that it could not have been—they could have set up the Panthers, but I rather doubt it. And in any organization, especially a law enforcement organization, if you're going to "set someone up," I think there would be someone in the police who wouldn't agree to that kind of thing. I think it would have come out then or strongly later.

QUESTION: What was the climate in the community after Dr. King was assassinated? How did the people feel about the police and about the Panthers? What was going through people's minds?

POLICEMAN: I think there was a lot of fear and paranoia in everyone's mind. A fear of the Panthers and the police. A fear of them coming down hard on everyone they could. And a fear in the honest citizen on the street. And needless to say, a lot of fear on the part of the policeman because of obvious hostility and ability of certain parts of society to enter into violence without even thinking twice about it.

QUESTION: Was the Black Panther headquarters near the campus?

POLICEMAN: It wasn't near the campus. It was near the Oakland-Berkeley line. We had plans on hand for an assault on that headquarters, if the need ever arose. We knew it was barricaded, and that there were weapons there. So we had plans drawn up—detailed plans.

QUESTION: Wasn't it possible when you knew that situation existed, like their hoarding a large cache of weapons, to get court permission to take it?

POLICEMAN: That becomes very difficult. I'm sure if they could have gotten the search warrant, or if they had enough cause to convince a judge there were illegal weapons in there, I'm sure they would have. But it was not illegal to have handguns, shotguns, or rifles in a given building. If we knew there were automatic weapons in that building, then you could have gotten a warrant and go in and seize the weapons. But unless you know that the person who lives there has been convicted of a felony and is in possession of a weapon, then you have no right to go in. You couldn't seize a legal weapon.

QUESTION: Do you remember having any contact with the Cleavers?

POLICEMAN: I was once in on an attempt to capture Kathleen Cleaver. There was a warrant out for her arrest and we had been given "want sheets" with pictures of Kathleen. I think this was after Cleaver had been incarcerated. There was a fairly high bail warrant out for her arrest. Our department, as well as others, were out looking for her. And it possibly wasn't that important a warrant, but trying to get her (in order) to get Cleaver. I don't remember whether this was before or after the shooting.

QUESTION: Did you feel Cleaver was a violent, inflammatory type; or a guy who was really trying to keep things cool when all that trouble was boiling?

POLICEMAN: I think he definitely was the moderate of

the Party and I think the man who was feared more was Newton. I think the general consensus was that Eldridge was the one who used his head and Newton was the warrior.

Panthers show their colors at the Alameda Court House

PIRKLE JONES

A PANTHER IS A BLACK CAT
Chapter 8

"... It is not a panther's nature to attack first, but when he is attacked and backed into a corner, he will respond viciously."

— Huey P. Newton

Some fascinating and important things led up to the April, 1968, gun battle. To get a "handle" on this microcosm of history and to better appreciate what was yet to come, we must look at what was happening during the few years leading up to it.

The night just before the end of the big march to Jackson sponsored by SNCC (the Student Nonviolent Coordinating Committee), Stokely Carmichael mounted a crude stage and called upon young blacks all over America to arm themselves for future conflict. He showed them the potential in black power. Immediately young blacks had a new cry. "Black power!" Here were words that finally meant something to them and after that no one could quiet the crowd.

Police and National Guardsmen took positions around the edges of the field. They handled their weapons nervously and the chanting grew louder. The shouts and taunts from whites which the marchers had endured for many days were now turned against the law. "White trash!" "Red-neck!"

One member of the Mississippi SNCC grabbed the microphone and threatened the whites in the crowd, "There are Black Panthers in the crowd from Lowndes County and they will blow your head clean off your body!"[1]

You could see an occasional policeman or guardsman

look furtively to the surrounding trees as if someone were lurking there. The black continued to taunt, "Oh, they is there, white boy, don't you worry about it, they is there." In catlike motions he acted out the movements of a panther and yelled, "I'm telling you, white boy, they is right there waiting for you. Panthers, Black Panthers, they is going to get you and then sneak off and wait for another white boy to kill."[2]

Headlines the next day spoke of "Black power!" Editorials discussed the possibility of a direct confrontation. Newscasters worried about black revenge.

To revolutionary blacks the distinctions between a Negro, "a nigger," a colored man, and a black are very real. To many whites, however, the terms seem synonymous and are used interchangeably. It is important to know what they mean to a black.

First, what is COLORED? A colored is one satisfied to let the racial situation remain status quo. A colored doesn't want to involve himself in bettering the black person's position. He is often called an "Uncle Tom."

Second, the long abusive term NIGGER. It is an offensive, derogatory word when used by the white man, a milder put-down when used by a black. Evolved from the French *nègre* and the earlier English *neger,* it embodies all of the prejudices of race differences.

Third, a NEGRO is a person who isn't happy with the present system and one who will take action. All his efforts, however, will be initiated through peaceful means—through the law. The NAACP and the Urban League may be examples of a "Negro" organization.

The term BLACK is today almost unilaterally used within the ranks of black America. This denotes a subjective awareness of all the unique qualities that result from being black. Skin color isn't all the term means. Still, "black" varies in its definition depending on one's perspective. To radicals, like the Panthers, if a black's "awareness" didn't generate militant activity, then his own use of the name black was synonymous with Negro.

Finally, the BLACK REVOLUTIONARY is a man who wants and fights for this "blackness." He is not satisfied to slowly reform society, it must be overthrown, completely changed. He will fight forcefully for an immediate change in the black situation. A Black Panther is a *black* cat. He is not a Negro or a colored person, he is black and extremely proud of it. He screams about the whites' racism while being a racist himself. The revolutionary doesn't think of his actions as being "lawless." He considers his role as something constructive, progressive and utterly positive for his people. The end justifies any means.

In the latter part of September, 1966, Huey Newton began to dictate his 10-Point Program for the Black Panther Party. The Party was officially launched on October 15, 1966, in a poverty program office within the black community at Oakland.

Here was Newton's 10-Point Panther Party platform and program:

1. We want freedom. We want power to determine the destiny of our black community.
2. We want full employment for our people.
3. We want an end to the robbery by the white man of our black community.
4. We want decent housing, fit for shelter of human beings.
5. We want education for our people that exposes the true nature of our true history and our role in the present-day society.
6. We want all black men to be exempt from military service.
7. We want an immediate end to police brutality and murder of black people.
8. We want freedom for all black men held in federal, state, county, and city prisons and jails.
9. We want all black people when brought to trial to be tried in court by a jury of their peer group or people from their black communities, as defined by the Constitution of the United States.

10.   . . . And as our major political objective, a United
        Nations supervised plebiscite to be held throughout
        the black colony in which only black colonial
        subjects will be allowed to participate, for the
        purpose of determining the will of black people as to
        their national destiny.[3]

Bobby Seale explained point 10 like this, "We, the Black
Panther Party, made great efforts to organize an element
which radical writer Frantz Fanon termed the 'lumpen
proletariat.' " Seale picked up on Fanon's thinking and put
it in his own language. "If you didn't relate to these cats,
the power structure will organize these cats against you."[4]
Blacks had better organize blacks.

Besides revolutionaries like Marx, Lenin, Mao and
Fanon, the Panthers, surprisingly enough, were influenced
by the lyrics of Bob Dylan. Several key Panthers listened to
the folk-rock hit, "Ballad of a Thin Man," with its typical
Dylan symbolism, while getting out the first *Black Panther*
newspaper. Its philosophy was to become a big part of their
whole publishing operation. Here's a bit of Dylan's lengthy
ballad:

"You hand in your ticket
And you go watch the geek
Who immediately walks up to you
When he hears you speak
And says how does it feel
To be such a freak?
And you say impossible
As he hands you a bone.

Because something is happening here
But you don't know what it is. . .
Do you, Mister Jones?"

The symbolic Mr. Jones is a typical bourgeois W.A.S.P.,
who takes a trip to a "carnival" to watch the geek—to

watch the unfortunate perform. To his astonishment, the geek calls him the freak! The carnival can represent any ghetto in America where Mr. Jones takes his youngsters to gawk at prostitutes, junkies and derelicts. Watching from inside his Cadillac, he hears: "But who is the real freak? Something is happening here, but you don't know what it is . . . do you, Mr. Jones?"

Bobby Seale told how the Dylan words were listened to and gained meaning: "These brothers would get halfway high, loaded or something, and they would sit down and play this record over and over and over, especially after they began to hear Huey Newton interpret that record. They'd be trying to relate an understanding about what was going on, because old Bobby (Dylan) did society a big favor when he made that particular sound."[5]

From May through October of 1967, it was a summer of racial disturbances. More than 40 riots took place, and at least 100 other major incidents. One result of those '67 riots was the strengthening of militant black groups across the nation.

One Panther said, "We floated around the streets, and we patrolled pigs. We followed pigs. They wouldn't even know we'd be following them . . . trying to catch them wrong . . . we'd just drive around behind them, a long time."[6]

One of the more controversial programs the Panthers began working on was their *Breakfast for Children* project. This, combined with their *Liberation School,* was designed to politically indoctrinate, as well as feed the youngsters. The food was sometimes expropriated from merchants who, the Panthers rationalized, were exploiting the community anyway.

The curriculum of the Liberation School was based on "experiences of revolutionaries that the children can relate to." The weekly program was built around daily topics, for example:

Monday is revolutionary history day
Tuesday is revolutionary culture day

Wednesday . . .
And so forth

The program, however, was not simply mild and academic. These impressionable school age children, second, third and fourth grades, were fed not only breakfast (often in church basements), but massive doses of racist propaganda. A coloring book showing blacks mutilating "pigs" (policemen) with guns, knives, and hatchets was distributed in at least five different programs. Children also marched to songs that told of "the pigs running amuck, and Panthers fighting for the people."[7] Perhaps lyrics such as these by Evette Pearson were used in the school:

"Our Father (says white America),
Which art in heaven,
How I love this game.
Of all the blessings
You've given me —
This game of pain
Is closest to my heart,
I said I'd pray and pray
You gave me the U.S.A.
I joined the trustee board
You let me kill the injuns, Lord
You blessed me with slaves
You blessed me with fools —
Then the niggers started going to schools.
Integration! Freedom!
Now it's revolution!
But I know
The Lord is Good
Your grace is sufficient to silence niggers
For good.
Amen!" [8]

Volatile Huey Newton couldn't control his temper and was repeatedly "mixing it up" with people at the slightest provocation. Seale tells about one of the Panthers' early confrontations. The Panthers had volunteered to guard Betty Shabazz, a dignitary visiting Cleaver (then with *Ramparts Magazine*), and in the process got into a skirmish with television cameramen trying to cover her.

Seale wrote, "A big beefy cop moved forward. He had unhooked the strap off of the hammer of his pistol, and started shouting at Huey, who said, 'Don't point that gun at me! Stop pointing that gun at me!'

"The cop kept making gestures as though he was going to go for his gun. Huey stopped in his tracks and just stared at the cop. Then he walked right up to within a few feet of him and said, 'What's the matter, you got an itchy finger?' The cop didn't say a thing. He just stood there.

" 'You want to draw your gun?' Huey asked him. The other pigs were calling for this one cop to cool it, but he didn't seem to hear them. He was looking right at Huey, staring straight into Huey's eyes.

"Newton said, 'Okay, you big fat racist pig, draw your gun!' The cop didn't move. 'Draw it, you cowardly dog!' And with that, Huey jacked a round off into the chamber of his own shotgun. 'I'm waiting,' Huey said, and, man, he just stood there waiting for this pig to make a move toward his gun. All of the other cops moved back out of the line of fire. The five of us were spread out behind Huey.

"Finally the fat pig just gave up. He let out a great big sigh and just hung his head. Huey almost laughed in his face, and we started backing up slowly. Huey backed up. Then the cops started talking about, 'Don't go for your guns. Don't you go for your guns.' So Huey said, 'Don't you go for your guns.'

"I remember repeating behind Huey, I said, 'That's right, don't you go for your guns. Don't you touch your guns.' I had flipped the little strap that went over the handle of my .38. So we were standing there, backing up, stepping off from the pigs, and the pigs were all bunched up.

"If just one of them had gone for his gun, he would blast him, because Huey had his gun at a 45-degree angle to the ground and he was ready. He had the barrel of the gun in his left hand. His finger was on the trigger, he had knocked the safety off, and he jacked a round off into the chamber. It kind of shook the cops when Huey jacked that round off in that chamber.

"We were stepping off and the cops took three or four steps forward. Then they stopped and realized that we had them. We backed across the street and stopped the traffic coming off and onto the ramp to the Bay Bridge. Traffic was jammed up. I know people in the cars were sitting there wondering what in the hell was going on. 'Who in the hell are these niggers with these guns, and the cops all on the streets. . . .' "[9]

ROOTS

Away back in July, 1847, Dred Scott, a black resident of Missouri, brought suit in a federal court for his freedom. Ten years later his case finally reached the Supreme Court. Then-Chief Justice Roger Taney ruled that "People of African descent are not and cannot be citizens of the United States, and that black people have no rights which whites are bound to respect."

It seemed too much—a last straw for even the Creator who through Isaiah had written, "Now the Lord saw . . . and it was displeasing in His sight that there was no justice."

Although the Dred Scott action took place 120 years ago, this kind of prejudicial behavior of some Americans still continued to provide fuel for the burning souls of black radicals like Bobby Seale. Seale told an audience of young whites in New York, "We hate you white people! And the next time one of you paddies comes up here and accuses me of hating you because of the color of your skin, I will kick you in your ---. We started out hating you because of the color of your skin. . . . In school, when a little white liberal walked by, I used to come up with my knife and say, 'Give me your lunch money or I'll cut your guts out.'

"Pretty soon I'd say, 'Tomorrow you bring me two

76

dollars.' And the next day he'd bring me two dollars, because that two dollars was mine. Mine because of 400 years of racism and oppression. When I take two dollars from you pigs, don't you say nothing!"[10]

But even the white radicals listening couldn't stomach Seale's blatant racism. One wrote in *Rat Subterranean News,* an underground New York newspaper, how he felt. "You (Seale) are denying my humanity," the writer said. "Though I am in deepest empathy with you and with all blacks—all people—in their struggle to be free, you are in danger of becoming my enemy. I must revolt against your racism, your scorn of everything white, just as I revolt against the racism of white America . . . I don't feel white enough or guilty enough to die joyfully by a bullet from a black man's gun, crying 'absolved at last!' "[11]

In Huey Newton's early years at Oakland's Tech High School an unfortunate incident occurred. One afternoon after his physical education class, a teacher thoughtlessly shouted out before showers, "The last one is a nigger baby!" Everyone took off running for the showers, all except one. Huey Newton never forgot that incident. It helped open the gates to a man and an organization that a lot of people will not easily forget.

Cleaver's first encounter with the Black Panthers was, as he put it, "love at first sight." It happened one night at a meeting of black activists in San Francisco's black ghetto.

Cleaver wrote of that first experience, "Suddenly the room fell silent. . . . There was only the sound of the lock clicking as the front door opened, and then the soft shuffle of feet moving quietly toward the circle. Shadows danced on the walls. From the tension showing on the faces of the people before me, I thought the cops were invading the meeting. But there was a deep female gleam leaping out of one of the women's eyes that no cop could ever elicit. I recognized that gleam out of the recesses of my soul, even though I had never seen it before . . . the total admiration of a black woman for a black man. I spun around in my seat and saw the most beautiful sight I had ever seen: Four black men wearing black berets, powder-like shirts, black leatherjackets, black trousers, shiny black shoes—and each with a gun! Where was my mind at? Blown!"[12]

One night, early in 1967, Huey was listening to the radio. What he heard struck a kindred chord. Huey and Bobby Seale drove right down to the radio station that night to meet "the voice" on the other end of their radio: Eldridge Cleaver.

Huey pleaded with Cleaver, "Man, look, you got to be in the Party! We need you! We want you!" Huey Newton has said, "I had asked Cleaver to join the Party a number of times." But he did not join until after that confrontation with the police in front of *Ramparts Magazine,* where the police were afraid to go for their guns.

Newton considered Cleaver, who was just coming out of prison, to be a new Malcolm X. Huey knew Cleaver was a brilliant communicator and that was exactly what the Panthers needed. But Cleaver himself wanted to do more than talk and write. He would rather pick up, somehow, the fallen mantle of Malcolm X.

It wasn't long before Cleaver was standing with Newton and Seale preening before a mirror in his apartment, wearing his own black leatherjacket and a beret.

He went on to become, as Chairman Bobby Seale put it, "One of the key brothers in the Black Panther Party. Of all the brothers on the Central Committee, Cleaver was the key brother."[13] David Hilliard indicated that Cleaver possessed "a strong personality and was able to dominate the Central Committee and Party philosophy."[14] Some believe Cleaver began to take on a messianic complex about his new mission.

Newton writing about this era said, "We were trying to build a political vehicle through which the people could express their revolutionary desires."

Newton, Seale and Cleaver began to fashion an organization to channel black rage into a revolution; to organize a weapon for use against what they loathed—white society. An early Panther member of the New York chapter remembers eagerly absorbing that "the police department was the first line of the racist U.S. government, and that all effort must be concentrated on liberating the 'occupied' black communities from them."[15]

He said, "It was easy to get black youth to identify their problems with hatred for the police and hating police was easy for me too. Stories about the Mississippi police beating marchers was still tearing at my mind. I had pledged revenge. I remembered a brother describing the way the panther moves quickly and quietly, how it strikes before anyone realizes what has happened.

"I thought, 'That's the way I'll be. I'll be a panther—a deadly Black Panther!' "[16]

Eldridge Cleaver — down or up?

CLEAVER FOR PRESIDENT
Chapter 9

A serious student of Cleaver may ponder whether something "snapped inside," April 6, the day of the shootout. As though some erratic thing arose in that place where he lived, pulsing over the following six years between possession and obsession. Certainly the man described by the Berkeley cop as "a moderate" appeared far from moderate on April 6, and for some time thereafter.

In the quest for understanding and accuracy, the author worked to digest more than a million words, written and spoken, by and about Cleaver. In carefully studying his tracks you cannot escape the fact that his behavior shifted! Rather suddenly he was acting out of character and it commenced sometime during that April afternoon.

Oh, there were continued similarities with the Cleaver of the past. But, unmistakably, there were differences too, and his change seems to follow right on through until the sixth year of his exile. An exile that began later in 1968. Increasingly, from that afternoon, Cleaver displayed certain paranoid behavior. His language dipped to a new low of repetitious obscenities. His brilliant and analytical mind showed evidences of staggering. Cleaver became obsessed with the establishment; with Ronald Reagan; Nixon and Humphrey; with anarchy and above all obsessed about "pigs." We might say he came down with acute pigitis. The evidences of Cleaver's own kind of moderation and softness just seemed to vanish from the afternoon of the gun battle.

The Cleaver who had steadied the blacks in northern California for two whole days after King's assassination was suddenly manifesting a different personality.

But meanwhile . . .

During the months of his being paroled and carrying right

on through the '68 Presidential elections, Cleaver seemed uncontrollably strident. In his huge meetings on the campuses and in the cities across the country he harangued as though driven by the devil himself and this hate traveled along with him to Havana, then right on to Algiers.

Cleaver didn't have to "snap." He let himself be victimized by that "Lawless One" he had unwittingly served since a boy. You can't turn on with drugs, confess hatred for years on end against everything and everybody and get away with it permanently. Cleaver was getting burnt by the hot acid steaming from his own pen and mouth. The Book of books says, "Out of the abundance of the heart the mouth speaketh." Cleaver's words and now his actions bore a malevolence he had nourished inside his heart.

In 1968 it wasn't just Humphrey and Nixon running for President but also—Eldridge Cleaver. Pigs became the favorite campaign theme, of course.

Bobby Seale credits Cleaver for creation of the term "pig." It proved to be a deadly semantic weapon.

Cleaver's Vice-Presidential running mate, Jerry Rubin, can shed some light on their campaign. Yes, it was the same Rubin who coined the snide spelling Amerika. Rubin writes in his book, *Do It!:* "Eldridge wanted an alliance between bad blacks and bad whites. Criminals of all colors to unite.... a quality-under-the-pigs ... Eldridge wanted a coalition between the Panthers and the psychedelic street activists. He had one requirement for his Vice-Presidential candidate: He had to be out on bail!"

Rubin continues, "I had just been attacked in my apartment by three New York narcs. So Eldridge called me, and I dug it. But what would the Peace and Freedom Party say?

"These whites can accept running a pot-smoking, gun-toting, ex-con nigger for President.

"But a long-hair, white, freak for Vice-President? ...

"I went to the New York convention of the Peace and Freedom Party and threw my hat in the ring...

"Eldridge was the craziest Presidential candidate America's ever seen."

On the steps of Sproul Hall, he led 5,000 Berkeley students in a shocking chorus; he did it again in a Catholic girls' school! The chorus was very obscene involving then-California governor, Ronald Reagan.

Jerry Rubin continued, "At the Panther-Yippie Election Day Rally Eldridge smoked a joint, poured out his soul to 3,000 people, and then withdrew his name from the Presidential campaign in favor of Pigasus. . . .

"When the movement moved into the streets and began to act in the dialect of power, when the movement got tough, he broke away all those barriers preventing us from reaching the average guy. America understands Cleaver. . . ." And that was the Vice-Presidential candidate's recollections of their campaign.

Then from the podium of Stanford Memorial Theater, Presidential candidate Cleaver spoke for 76 minutes to a packed house with 800 more listening outside. Cleaver described the United States as a successor to Nazi Germany, the No. 1 obstacle to human progress, and called her by his favorite coined name, "Babylon."

Speaking of China's Mao Tse-tung, candidate Cleaver said, "Baby, you've done a beautiful job."

Cleaver said, "Ronald Reagan is a punk, a sissy and a coward; and I challenge him to a duel to the death or until he says 'Uncle Eldridge.' I give him a choice of weapons: a gun, a knife, a baseball bat or marshmallows."

Yes, their campaign was that profound!

Years later from Algiers, in response to Jerry Rubin's invitation to write an introduction for Rubin's revolutionary book *Do It!* Cleaver wrote, in part: "On the night of October 27, 1967, in the wee, wee hours of the darkness, guns blazed in the heart of black Oakland on 7th and Willow Streets. The quiet of the night was shattered by the minor thunder of the guns. Death was stalking a circle around warring men, and the shadow of death was created by the blaze leaping from the barrel of a gun. A pig white lay dead, deep fried in the fat of his own —— and another pig white lay there, similar to the dead one in every respect, except that he did not die. This was a rare moment of death for the oppressor and triumphant for the oppressed. This beautiful spark of glory on the streets in the dark in Babylon lights the way for 'lil Bobby' to find room in which to die a warrior's death, and light to show those who remain and fight on how to finish the job of offing the pigs."

In the flashing gutter-eloquence of Cleaver's pen, you may feel a giant threshing to break out of the corpse in which he was still choosing to live.

A few last parting volleys from Mr. Cleaver for President: He didn't exactly dream of walking in the White House after the November election. "If through some quirk of circumstances, I would have been elected President, I would not have entered the White House, but I would have burned it down. . . ." The campaign was really an organizing effort to get revolutionary blacks and whites working together. "A group of our leaders blew in for a meeting at the United Nations to apply for status as a 'non-governing organization' and asked for the U.N. to station observers in every negro community in America."

"Adam Clayton Powell is a political prostitute, and we're going to get rid of him. He's not militant enough."[5]

Cleaver was defeated for President of the United States by a mere 60 million votes. The Cleaver-Rubin ticket somehow lost the entire "pig" vote.

The race was over and Cleaver came face to face with his future. His decision: imprisonment or flight.

In the next chapter, we will follow Cleaver from the scene of the shootout, which he miraculously survived, to jail from which he was again paroled, by a "miraculous" court decision, and through his subsequent exile.

°Cleaver for president, with Police calling cards

THE ODYSSEY
Chapter 10

"Dear brothers in Vietnam,
Either quit the Army now, or start destroying it from
the inside. You need to start killing the racist pigs
who are over there giving you orders. Kill General
Abrams and his staff. Especially the Uncle Tom
officers should be dealt with, because the pigs will use
them as effective tools against our people.
Cleaver"[1]

Bobby Hutton and Cleaver left from the Oakland
shootout in different cars—Cleaver to the San Quentin
infirmary and Bobby to the morgue!

The San Quentin warden thought Cleaver was too hot to
handle. His presence might unhinge some of the other
prisoners. So he quickly moved him on up to Vacaville
Prison to continue his recuperation. And that's where he
stayed locked up for nearly two months until June 6, 1968,
when Judge Raymond Sherwin of Solano County ordered
him to be released on grounds that Cleaver had, in fact,
been jailed for political reasons.

Three parole violations had been claimed: possession of
firearms, associating with individuals of bad repute, and
failure to cooperate with a parole officer.

Judge Sherwin noted that Cleaver's only handling of a
firearm was "in obedience to a police command"; that no
individuals of bad reputation were specifically identified,
only "the Black Panther Party"; and that "the uncon-
tradicted evidence presented to this Court indicated that
the petitioner has been a model parolee."

The cancellation of Cleaver's parole, concluded Judge
Sherwin, "was the product of a type of pressure un-

becoming, to say the least, to the law enforcement paraphernalia of this State."

David Hilliard and Kathleen drove up to Vacaville to bring the newly released Cleaver back to San Francisco.

For so many years now he has been volatile, creative, energetic and, above all, talkative. He has written so much, been talked about so much, been interviewed so often and made so much news that his big tracks are easy for any historian to follow.

As a matter of fact, an interviewer during the years in exile once asked him, "What do you consider your biggest failings, the things about yourself you must work hardest to overcome?"

Cleaver shot back, "Talking too much! I'm a fat mouth, you know."[2]

And still earlier he had been asked what his end objectives were.

Cleaver answered, "Is there anything really wrong with utopia? . . . What we want to do is to bring heaven down to earth, you see. That is, to create the best possible living conditions that human knowledge and technology are capable of providing. That's the aspiration of the revolutionary, and that's the dream. So I'm saying that ideologically our hope indicates a socialist America—a communist America."[3]

An irony of the upheavals of the '60s is the fact that charitable motives were underlying what some of the radicals attempted to do. To be fair we must recognize this fact. Some radicals and some establishment people wanted the same thing for America but they were coming at solutions from different perspectives. A dangerous polarity was developing—the kind that has destroyed other countries. Everyone wanted heaven, but they were conflicting in the means to bring it about. It is the responsibility of both the right and left to be on guard against destructive polarities building up. The nation is worth this discipline.

But a malevolence in Cleaver's soul started way back at

about 11 or 12. Like a rising fury, even his teen years were full of vandalism, petty crimes, drugs, and later, even rape. His last year in high school was the tenth-grade. He later received not only his high school diploma at San Quentin, but also picked up his "doctorate in revolution."

One of the many things being honed at an early age was a disdain and hatred for what he fancied to be the hypocrisy of preachers, churches and Christians. Even when clapped in solitary confinement, where a Bible was the only book, he would have no part of it.

But now Cleaver was out and racing through the country again. He used the last of his free time in America as if anointed by old Satan himself. His actions and his sheer survival from the shootout had electrified the left and rocketed him into high orbit. Now Cleaver was an instant superstar with a scent of immortality. Three thousand, 5,000 and even 10,000 students were turning out on campuses and in auditoriums straining for every word from their latter-day hero. Along with his diabolical anointing, he must also have gotten a foul spirit, gratis. This bright, highly articulate man was now monotonously spewing filthy, obscene words. He became so foul-mouthed that even Huey Newton sent word from his prison cell ordering Cleaver to clean up his language.

When he was born in 1935 to Leroy and Thelma Cleaver in Wabbaseka, Arkansas, they certainly didn't foresee a bad-mouthed genius. Shortly after little Eldridge was born his parents moved on to Phoenix, Arizona. His daddy began to work on the Super Chief and from there the family moved to Pasadena, California. There, Cleaver's parents separated and his mother went to work for the Los Angeles school system.

The boy was in junior high school when he was first arrested. It was during his stretch in reform school at nearby Whittier that he learned to hustle marijuana. This time in reform school (or as Huey Newton put it, in Crime School) proved to be a "soul breaker." It was there, while locked in, Cleaver's soul first began to ice.

Soon he had climbed to Soledad Prison, then all the way up to "Big Q." Along the way Cleaver's convict "professors" stamped their marks on his pliable, young mind.

It was also in prison where his unquenchable thirst developed for books on philosophy, socialism, Rosicrucianism, leftist politics, Muslim religion and flat-out revolution. And Cleaver drank deeply. Nobody made him read these books or do the things he did. Cleaver always made clear he was his own man, master of his own fate, captain of his own soul.

Yet, in the fall, the California Appeals Court finally overruled Judge Sherwin's ruling on the writ of habeas corpus. Cleaver was ordered back to prison within 60 days—by the 27th of November, to be exact. (He still faces a possible maximum of 70 years in jail if convicted.) Cleaver firmly believed that if he went back to prison he would be a dead man. Again Eldridge was recently quoted as saying, "One thing I'm not going to apologize for is leaving this country. Then I was convinced if I had gone back to San Quentin I wouldn't have walked out of there alive. Subsequent events haven't changed that opinion."

Several days before his secret flight from the U.S., Cleaver addressed a San Francisco meeting called to help meet the financial needs for the legal fight ahead. It turned out to be his final U.S. public appearance. As officers entered his Oakland apartment, November 27, Cleaver was watching the event on television in Canada.

Cleaver's international odyssey had begun. Now, he would be able to see with his own eyes the politics he had been advocating at work in real live showcases of communist and socialist nations.

Still, with all his cool bravado, Cleaver had been experiencing deep apprehensions in the month before he fled through Canada. It's there to be read between the lines in his October *Playboy* interview of that year. "I couldn't conceive of myself playing any other role—not even if I have to go back to prison for it. I'm going to do everything I can not to go back to prison, but I can't compromise my beliefs. I'd rather be dead than do that. And I may have a violent end, anyway. I'm hearing more and more these days from people telling me to be careful. . . ."

Thanks to that "assist" by old Judge Sherwin it became easy for Cleaver to slip out of the country and decline the waiting hospitality of the "San Quentin Hilton." As every year ticked off and with each new communist "paradise" visited, Cleaver grew more and more shaken at the absence of the very freedoms Marxist ideology boasts about. Freedom, supposedly Marxism's glorious end-product, he found to be a lie. The truth was that they were the world's most repressive societies, subjecting their own people to suffering, and shockingly, "Their people had no opportunity to influence the direction of their countries."

After surfacing in Canada, Cleaver was next sighted in Havana which he had, in fact, reached by ship despite one AP story which had him "a passenger on a plane that someone else had hijacked with a toy gun."

Fidel Castro's Cuba quickly set him up in lavish style. As a reward for tweaking Uncle Sam's beard, Cleaver was given the luxury penthouse apartment of an exiled Dr. Rafael Reineke. The big, plush apartment included two large terraces, one looking to the city, the other to the sea.

What Cleaver saw, heard and felt in this first communist showcase was bitter disappointment. Cleaver and another Panther, airline skyjacker named Johnson, began to slip messages out of Havana to Black Panther members about their discontent. Their indictment against Castro was summed up in a few words, in effect, "We don't like the unrevolutionary way we are being treated. We don't like the treatment of black revolutionaries and the Black Panthers here at all."

It was a short honeymoon!

Then, when Reuters News Agency broke the story that Cleaver was in Cuba and when some embarrassing gossip broke in the Havana papers involving a girl, "kind hearted" Fidel insisted Cleaver take a little vacation.

Cuban officials broke the news to Cleaver by promising

him that the long delay in allowing his wife to join him was about to end.

"You are going to meet your wife."

"Where?"

"In Algeria."

"I don't want to go to Algeria."

"You can return at a later time."

There was no use in Cleaver's arguing. A photographer was taking his picture for documents. A tailor was measuring him for clothes when he was handed his free ticket—one way.

A few days later a frustrated Cleaver was set up in a tiny room on the fourth floor of the old Victoria Hotel in the Arab quarters of downtown Algiers. "The toilet and shower are just down the hall, thank you." To complicate things a very, very pregnant Kathleen arrived frazzled with weariness and tension. There wasn't a kitchen or even a restaurant in the whole seedy Victoria.

In spite of the discomforts it was during his years in Algiers that Cleaver's evolution to a fully committed Marxist-Leninist was completed. Over the next several years he became more obsessed with the evils of America, "What the U.S.A. needs is a Yankee-Doodle-Dandy brand of socialism."

Columnist and scintillating wit, William Buckley, recently, bitingly described Cleaver as "the godfather of the Black Panther organization . . . who began his career by doing time for rape and robbery, got out on bail, involved himself in a shootout in which his companion was killed, then jumped bail and went to the free world to escape further persecution by the pigs. His free world began in Cuba where after a few months he noticed in the discrimination-free land of Cuba, all generals were white, and all privates were black. He went on, like Candide; to Algeria this time, where he was received as a hero and treated like a prisoner."

Man Without a Country

Cramped accommodations and all, it was in Algiers

where the Cleavers' first child Maceo, a baby boy, was born. And also, it was during the years in Algiers when he eventually put Marxism under the high-powered microscope of his mind, and from where Cleaver spread an international network of the Panther Party. During this era he was darting back and forth to about every African capital, third world capital and communist nation on earth. He received a stream of emissaries from world leaders and radical groups. He claimed to have been politically involved with those who overturned the regimes in Angola, Mozambique, and others. Cleaver was truly a king without a castle.

But the restless sleep and troubling dreams that he had tried to live with since 18 started to get more acute. Cleaver began to feel increasingly suffocated in Algiers and started looking across the Mediterranean toward France for more "air space." His visits to Marxist utopias in North Korea, Moscow, China had been no holiday. Was that icy soul starting to thaw?

The harder he squinted into his microscope at the hammer and sickle the more evident it became that its redness was from the blood of its own people. Was he becoming a burned-out revolutionary? Cleaver's 20-year Marxist dream seemed in its death rattle.

His own country apparently terminally cut off, the best substitute he could think of was France. Six years had passed. Cleaver had intently followed rapid and startling changes that were taking place in America. The Vietnam war had finally ended. Watergate had shaken the country. The U.S. hadn't collapsed and some things unforeseen were happening. Black people were being voted into high offices, even being commissioned generals.

Cleaver began to make plans for that move to France, where, from a balcony overlooking the Mediterranean, he would soon have an experience so shattering it would ignite his icy soul.

Eldridge with son Antonio Maceo, age 7, named after a black Cuban revolutionary, and daughter Joju, age 6. (Joju was named by the wife of Communist Korea's premier during Cleaver's odyssey).

KATHLEEN, MY LOVE
Chapter 11

One key to understanding a man is to meet the woman in his life. What part, if any, did Cleaver's wife, Kathleen, play in his role as a Black Panther, as a fugitive, as a man-come-home?

Eldridge Cleaver scratched a vivid mark on the pages of recent history. His path has been ragged: prisons, shoot-outs, the life of the hunted. A woman willing to join in such a volatile, fear-streaked life-style would require a rare blend of passion and loyalty.

Cleaver's woman, Kathleen, came from a diverse back-ground. Her father, Dr. Ernest Neal, was a college professor. She grew up a member of the black bourgeoisie in a number of college towns including Tuskegee, Alabama.

Later, when Dr. Neal joined the foreign service, little Kathleen went along to live in New Delhi, the Philippines, Liberia, and in Sierra Leone. An honor student in American schools abroad, she returned to attend the George School, a Quaker boarding school in Bucks County, Pennsylvania.

The next stop in her education was Oberlin College, founded as a theological institute a century earlier by America's greatest revivalist, Charles Grandison Finney. Finney, one of the most powerful orators ever to stand behind a pulpit, vigorously opposed slavery in any form. Although in his day openly criticized, he refused to support or even teach at Oberlin unless human beings of all colors were permitted to study God's Word freely and equally. Surely, it meant an interesting educational step for Kathleen.

After Oberlin, and a short period of government work in Washington, Kathleen was enrolled in Barnard, a swank women's college in the east. At Barnard she stayed but one semester because, while there, Kathleen discovered the civil rights movement. This attracted her far more than the drab formal education.

She said, "I was learning things there that I was not learning in school. I began to get educated in the true sense—to relearn things about the system, and I developed a new ideological perspective—a black perspective."

The semester's end found her in the SNCC (Student Non-Violent Coordinating Committee) office in New York. Shortly thereafter she went to Atlanta as SNCC's Campus Program Secretary. In March of '67 she organized a black students' conference in Nashville. It was here she was to have an encounter which redirected her entire life. Kathleen met Eldridge Cleaver.

It happened on the ground of old Fisk College, where Cleaver had been invited as guest speaker. Immediately he struck her as an eloquently lucid speaker, as well as a tremendously handsome and magnetic person. "What startled me most about him was that he referred to himself as a 'convict'! Seeing him at the conference as he moved about with supreme confidence, an ease that approached elegance, and a dignified reserve that all combined to give him an air that could best be described as stately, it seemed hard to conceive of this powerful man as a 'convict.' He exuded strength, power, force in his very physical being. To think of such a man caged up and designated for the dung heap of history was impossible. In my blissful ignorance, Eldridge Cleaver seemed as remote from prison as the moon; he walked the earth like a King."

After this encounter with the "charismatic" young black leader, an enraptured Kathleen, while airborne from Nashville to Washington, wrote a passionate love poem to Cleaver entitled, "My King, I Greet You." It was her own answer to his open letter from *Soul on Ice*, "To all black women from all black men" entitled "My Queen, I Greet You."

Not long thereafter, the Angela Davis look-alike came to San Francisco and began functioning as Communications

Secretary for the Black Panther Party. In December of 1967 Kathleen and Eldridge were married. They moved into an apartment on Oak Street in San Francisco. A short time later, on the night of January 6, the San Francisco police tactical squad came bursting in. Whatever they were looking for (probably a gun) they didn't find it. But Kathleen had an educational experience and a taste of things to come.

When Cleaver first joined the Party, Huey Newton let it be known that Cleaver was not to possess a weapon because he was an ex-felon. The Party set this policy, to avoid wasting its resources in unnecessary legal activities. Cleaver followed Newton's order and didn't himself have guns. However, one night after a frightening police raid on their apartment Kathleen asked him, "What if we actually got attacked and didn't have anything to defend ourselves with?" After a long discussion, Kathleen went to the store and bought a gun, all faithfully reported to Cleaver's parole officer.

Cleaver and the Panthers were fast becoming a thorn in the Bay area police departments' flesh. Confrontations were multiplying and taking on an increasingly ugly appearance. That education of Kathleen's was continuing. Her husband and the man that the police thought they knew seemed to be two different men.

"After I met him at the Fisk conference and got to know him a little, I was surprised by his tenderness. Expecting him to be harsh and cold from his experiences, instead, I found Eldridge to be amazingly warm, kind, gentle and sensitive. And as we came to know each other well, fell in love, got married and began working together, I watched Eldridge continue to grow, to develop, and to improve himself. His capacity for regeneration seemed boundless. One of Eldridge's greatest talents is the ability to see another person's latent strengths and abilities and bring them to the surface, making that person stronger and more competent than he ever thought he could be."

Kathleen remembers that on April 6, her husband spoke

at a rally on the Sproul Hall steps at Berkeley. "We were walking up Telegraph Avenue toward the campus. The sun was shining brightly and as I looked at Eldridge, with his black leatherjacket gleaming in the sun, his black sweater, black pants, black shoes, black hair and black sunglasses, walking deliberately and thoughtfully up the street, he seemed to be cloaked in death!"

She felt an overpowering sense of dread that she could neither explain nor articulate; the thought flashed through her mind that this was the last time she would ever see Eldridge. That night Eldridge was indeed involved in a near-brush with death.

Kathleen said, "That night I was waiting for Eldridge to come get me from a friend's house in Berkeley. We watched the 11 o'clock news and a report came on about a shootout with the Oakland police, but no names, no time, no location was given. I remembered my earlier premonition and shuddered! But I pushed it out of my mind again. I finally fell asleep on the couch by the phone. Many people tried to call me that night but I slept through the calls as if I were drugged. At 5:00 a.m., I finally awoke to receive a call from attorney Alex Hoffman. He told me that Eldridge was in San Quentin and Bobby Hutton was dead!"

She finally saw Eldridge at 11:00 a.m., on April 7, in the Vacaville California Medical Facility. He was in a wheelchair, completely covered with burns, bruises and cuts, and his foot was bandaged. His face was bloated from tear gas and his eyes were swollen out of shape. His hair and beard were matted. The guards wheeled him into the attorney's room from his cell. She said, "I watched through the glass windows as he was wheeled down the hall—he looked like a captured giant, a battered war casualty, a caged King! During the past few months Eldridge had begun to refer to himself as the Minister of Information, but now here he was again—a convict.

"He was so drugged that he could hardly keep his head up or his eyes open. I was reading the reports of the shootout to him from the *Oakland Tribune* and his head kept falling down. I put my arms around his shoulders to support his neck, and every time his head fell on my shoulder, I would kiss him lightly on the forehead. This incensed the guards watching outside; they came in and forced me to sit on the other side of the table. In prison, even a kiss from a wife is against the rule."

The two months Cleaver spent in Vacaville were a torture. Kathleen seemed to live the entire time in a state of suspended animation. Getting Eldridge out of prison was her sole concern. Then to the shock of everyone involved, Judge Raymond Sherwin granted a writ of habeas corpus on June 11, 1968. Cleaver was again to be freed.

"To me it seemed as if this were all a dream. I couldn't believe my eyes as I watched Eldridge being processed for release by the Solano County sheriff's office. They brought him down the hall where a crowd of people waited to witness this unprecedented event. The sun in the valley had tanned Eldridge to a crisp reddish brown; he was very lean, having lost weight in the penitentiary, and his beard and mustache had been shaven. He look 10 years younger, and as one friend put it, rather 'newborn'! We drove back to San Francisco and held a brief press-conference celebration in Garry's (Cleaver's attorney) office. When asked by reporters what his immediate plans were, he replied, 'I want to get reacquainted with my wife.'

"On September 27, the day Huey Newton was sentenced . . . the State Court of Appeals rendered its decision on Eldridge's release from Vacaville. It was devastating. He had 60 days to *return to prison!* The decision, which I thought I had been prepared to hear, left a deadened feeling in the pit of my stomach. There was no question in my mind about Eldridge's returning to prison; not only would it have been, as he said, the trip that breaks a man; but the trip would have destroyed me.

"What went on in Eldridge's mind once he heard the decision I never knew; he rarely discussed it. We could not discuss it. We could only act!

"I watched Eldridge daily grow increasingly tense,

harassed and paranoid. I saw less and less of him as his schedule became tighter—his time shorter. One day he bought himself an hourglass with blue crystals of sand which ran completely through in approximately 10 minutes. He appeared drained and exhausted. The pressure that was being exerted upon him could not be shared; it was a solitary burden, for no one else was named in the order to return to prison.

"His hair became grayer; his face became haggard; his shoulders began to sag. It was horrible to see the look of defeat begin to creep into his eyes, something I'd never seen . . . as long as I'd known him. I wouldn't see him for days on end. When he did come home, it would be in the morning to bathe, change his clothes, sometimes eat, and then leave. He became totally preoccupied with the work which he loved, and which he soon would have to stop.

"It is painful to recount these days, so painful my mind refuses to come up with the details. We lived a life with the beauty and joy of our love and work daily being crushed out and drained away by the pressure of—the deadline! I was so exhausted, both mentally, physically, and emotionally I was convinced I would be dead by the end of the month. Eldridge would never say what he was going to do other than refer to 'a showdown.' I silently begged him to leave; hundreds of friends and co-workers also hoped he would move to protect himself, and some openly told him he had to split."

He did.

Kathleen Cleaver was not to see her husband again until June 1969, in Algiers, where she arrived eight months pregnant. Kathleen, thinking her husband was in Cuba, was intercepted by writer-photographer Lee Lockwood in Paris. Lockwood had been sent as Cleaver's emissary with the urgent message that he had been asked to leave Cuba and was headed for Algeria.

The strain on Kathleen didn't vanish when she left the U.S. for Algeria. She did not find it to be the world's most accommodating nation, and especially so if you happened to be pregnant. Kathleen Cleaver, being "great with child," was suffering from a combination of physical exhaustion and tension, and confined to her bed most of the time. Since no restaurant or kitchen existed in the Victoria Hotel, Cleaver was forced to eat all his meals out. He would bring back food to Kathleen in a stack of interlocking aluminum pails he had bought in a sporting goods store. In addition, there was the nerve-wracking uncertainty about where Kathleen would have her baby, now due in a matter of weeks.

A few years later, in France, the Cleavers came to what he calls their dead end. "As far as children and family were concerned, the stresses and strains of our life abroad were intolerable. At first I was trying to force Kathleen to leave me. I knew it would be better for her and the children in the United States. I could only deal with that if I got mad at her and it was the same with her. She couldn't do it unless I drove her to it. So I was doing just that! But it wasn't something I wanted, that is where the depression came in. I really felt trapped."

Understandably there will be those who will bring up Cleaver's past indictment for rape and consider his present nobility toward women hypocritical. But before judgement is passed (and the author abhors the brutal, insidious and sick act of rape) it might be profitable to search for any signs of Cleaver's repentance—even back then.

Several statements in *Soul on Ice* reflecting on his sexual aggression, hint at a conscience not yet seared, "After I returned to prison, I took a long look at myself and, for the first time in my life, admitted that I was wrong, that I had gone astray—astray not so much from the white man's law as from being human, civilized—for I could not approve the act of rape. Even though I had some insight into my own motivations, I did not feel justified. I lost my self-respect. My pride as a man dissolved and my whole fragile moral structure seemed to collapse, completely shattered. We are a very sick country—I, perhaps, am sicker than most."

Cleaver, like any other person, should be gauged not on

what he was but rather on the man he now is. Once, while living in Algiers, Cleaver was asked whether he was looking forward to becoming a father. Manifesting a curious softness in the midst of an otherwise radical dialogue, he stuttered out, "Well, I don't know. I mean, I'm going through changes about that, you know. I'm very delighted about it. I didn't think that I would ever—somewhere inside me, you know, I've always wanted to be a father. I want a little boy. When I say that to Kathleen, she says I'm a male chauvinist. But if it's a little girl, I can dig it. Well, you know I'll be even more responsible, because—you see children are really the people that I dig."[1]

Kathleen Neal was in many ways remarkable before she met Eldridge, and now as Kathleen Cleaver, wife of one of America's most controversial figures, she has proven more remarkable. Kathleen has a dynamic image. She is not eclipsed. Her qualities shine from beyond the shadow of a great man. Of her forthrightness, no one who has had a meaningful encounter with her will ever question.

One reporter, who attended her Marin College appearance, wrote, "She addressed the audience with eloquence and with such obvious honesty, one had to believe her—besides she is stunning in her beauty."[2]

Recently, Kathleen read Watergate-figure Colson's best-selling book, "Born Again," and said it mellowed her own spiritual outlook.

Most notable, however, is the almost unbelievable loyalty and faithfulness of Kathleen to a husband not always free to provide for the needs and desires of his wife.

It appears the years of running may now be over for the Cleavers—possibly they are the wiser. During a recent television interview, Eldridge remarked, "Kathleen and I are one, and we've been together now for over seven years. We're united in wedlock and we've passed on the breath of life to our two children and we move together . . . we are now together, together forever!"[3]

That's one blessing the Cleavers will never again take for granted.

Vivacious Kathleen Cleaver

DAMASCUS ROAD
Chapter 12

Cleaver had said, "I attacked all forms of piety, loyalty, and sentiment: marriage, love, God, patriotism, the Constitution, the founding fathers, law, concepts of right-wrong-good-evil. ... Our atheism was a source of enormous pride to me. Later on, I bolstered our arguments by reading Thomas Paine and his devastating critique of Christianity."[1]

But the Epistle according to the new Eldridge started in the final year of his self-imposed exile in France. He had become increasingly disillusioned and increasingly overwhelmed with himself and the life he was trapped in. Perhaps out of desperation, he began to think *beyond* this world, even if fleetingly. Could there be anything beyond? he wondered. Death was something he had always dreaded. But after their first child, Cleaver had new thoughts—thoughts, he later said, that were about the vast and complicated universe out there. These thoughts were making him aware of the intelligent organization of the universe. Above all, he was beginning to understand that there were systems and designs from a brilliant intelligence somewhere. That there was that mysterious stream of life! And now, Kathleen and he had joined that ongoing stream. He knew, "There was nothing in the communist philosophies to explain that."[2]

But the realities and pressures of the *now* started to obliterate the early flashes from his frozen spirit and the "now" became an ominous cloud. He began to experience something that he had never had before—depression. Later, he explained, "I began to feel depressed, to be worried and a miserable companion to everyone around me. I went through a thing of trying to drive my wife away from me."[3]

Eldridge had heard, read and talked about depression in

the past, but he had never actually felt it. Now it gnawed at him, stifled love, threatened his marriage. Life itself seemed futile. He became obsessed with his own emptiness.

Kathleen seemed to understand what he was going through. She never threatened to leave him. She never condemned him for being the cause of their exile. She was there—if he needed her.

"I was miserable," Eldridge recalls. "Even during the nine years spent in prison, I never felt like I was beginning to feel." He saw that he was the only fugitive in his family. Kathleen had no arrest records, no "all-points" bulletin out for her. In fact, during the seven years they had been outside the country, she had been back and forth to the United States fairly regularly. Certainly, his children were innocent and could come and go. It was Cleaver himself who was the problem.

What weighed heaviest on his shoulders were his children, though. They were entered in the French educational system, and they had stopped speaking English. In fact, they wouldn't speak English. They spoke French, they played a kind of French football, they came home talking in French. Cleaver said that he tried to talk to them in English, making them listen to English records and trying to get them to read English books and printed matter because he wanted them to understand that they were Americans and that they weren't French. But they would say, "je suis francais; je suis francaise." The problem became big to him. He saw himself as the cause of their being locked outside of their country. Strangely enough, he felt the burden upon him because he wanted Maceo to play football!—but not the kind that was played in France. "I wanted him to play FOOTBALL like I used to play!"[4]

Cleaver went to the south of France, supposedly to work. He had found an apartment there on the Mediterranean, taken his books, papers, and files so he could work there on his manuscripts. But he would find himself brooding, becoming more and more miserable and restless.

Then he would rush back to Paris, and again end up causing problems for his wife.

One of these times when he was back in Paris, they sat down to a dinner that Kathleen had prepared. Candles were lighted on the table and the other lights turned off. His son, Maceo, sat on one side of the table, his daughter, Joju, on the other, and Kathleen was across from him.

"I was suddenly struck," Cleaver said, "by the realization that there was no light in our house—there was no light in our lives! There was no purpose in our lives, and there was no future for us."[5]

He got up from the table and made some excuses, then ran out of the house, and took another plane headed back for the south of France.

He found himself worried and utterly depressed. He was even thinking about taking his own life and ridding his family and the world of himself. He had never in his life felt so badly. He had been in prison nine years and had hated every minute of it, but he had never felt this deep weariness—this feeling of being at the end of his rope.

Later that night—about 10 o'clock—Cleaver was on the balcony. He looked up and saw the stars in the heavens.

"I thought about killing myself," he said. "At least my children and my wife could go back home and they would be free of that burden."[6]

He sat there, just looking up at the stars and at the shadows in the moon. He kept looking. First, he thought he saw sort of a man in the moon. It could have been the picture of himself which he had seen on many posters that had been used in the Black Panther Party—a profile of himself. It was! He looked at this moon image; strange feelings came over him. "I began to sweat and tremble," he later told, "and as I looked at this image, I saw consecutively the images of Fidel Castro, of Mao Tse-tung, of Karl Marx—my heroes.... Suddenly I saw an image of Jesus Christ! And this completely terrified me. When I saw that image—His eyes—something snapped back, and I began to

107

shake like a leaf and cry uncontrollably. I felt like I was just going to disintegrate."[7]

Some force outside himself made him fall down on his knees. He was trembling and crying. From somewhere came the memory of parts of the Lord's Prayer and the 23rd Psalm.

He began to recite over and over again, the 23rd Psalm, with some kind of feeling that this was the only way he could control his crying and the trembling. As he repeated it, the trembling finally subsided.

In his library was a copy of the Bible. It was the family Bible which his wife had brought when she joined him in Algeria. He remembered it and ran inside to get it. He turned quickly to the 23rd Psalm.

He read it and turned to other pages and he read until words began to swim before his eyes. "It had some real brilliant meaning to me because I felt that I was near death. I was in the valley of the shadow of death. I went inside and I layed down and went to sleep. I have never slept as soundly and peacefully as I slept that night."[8]

When he awoke the next morning, he saw his way back home. "It was just as clear in my mind as anything has ever been. I saw a trail or a path of light that ran right through a prison cell. I can see it now when I think about it, just as clearly as I saw it that morning. A prison cell that was open on one side and open on the other side, and light ran through it. The prison cell was like a dark spot in this path of life. And I understood instantly what it meant."[9]

He had to pass through the prison cell. It was the only way to resolve his problem. A prison cell was the last thing he ever wanted to see. But he understood that this was the solution—that beyond that prison cell was a beautiful life.

He did not jump up and rush back, but pondered about it for a couple of days. What had happened that night was a unique experience. Would it hold up with time? It did. He returned to Paris.

He didn't tell Kathleen right away but waited for the right moment. "I was sitting back on the bed and she was just looking at me. She knew something was different. Living with me, she expected almost anything, so she was kind of leery, you know.

"Finally she sat down and I told her that I'd decided to surrender, that we were going home. I watched her carefully, observing her reaction. It looked as though a great weight had just dropped away from her. I saw a radiance, a light, in her eyes I hadn't seen in a long time. That was what I was looking for—that clinched it for me! So I was at peace on that point from then on. We talked about it."[10]

Eldridge contacted his lawyers. They in turn contacted the Department of Justice. They organized his surrender. They got a guarantee of his security from the prison system and from the Oakland Police Department. It was the only "arrangement" involved. Everything else was left open-ended. He was to undergo the normal judicial procedures to resolve the residue of his legal problems.

All of this took time. For Eldridge, the weeks that went by seemed forever. He was impatient. He wanted it to happen now. He worried that he might change his mind. But he did not vacillate. His decision became more and more resolute. Then the lawyers finally got it all together. Eldridge went home.

When he got back, all kinds of people were wondering what happened. They asked, "Why did you do this?" One was an assistant minister (God Squad chaplain, George Stevens, of the Calvary Baptist Church) in San Diego, where Eldridge had been taken to the federal prison. Stevens had been a black militant during the '60s, and then had gone on to become a minister. He got permission to see Eldridge, and he brought a Bible with him.

Eldridge said, "I explained to him what I was thinking, how I was feeling inside, why I had gone, and why I had come back. He said, 'Eldridge, I understand.' He continued, 'I don't want you to respond right now to this. I just want you to listen. Let me do this—can I do this?'

"I told him, 'Yes.'

109

"He took the Bible and said, 'Eldridge, this is Jesus Christ.'

"Then he said, 'Jesus Christ, this is Eldridge Cleaver.' And that just zapped me! I got angry. I thought it was presumptuous of him to say that the way he said it; but it had the effect that he intended. It went straight to my heart! He went away and never did come back to see me."[11]

Later Eldridge was transferred to the Alameda County Jail in Oakland. There, ministers came in regularly. He began to listen to them as they talked to other prisoners. One day he told one of these ministers—his name was Glen Morrison—that he wanted to talk with him. Eldridge explained how he felt inside.

Morrison whispered, "That's the God-shaped vacuum that's in everybody. It can only be filled with Jesus Christ." He went on to share with Eldridge the Bible and the message of Jesus Christ as his personal Saviour. It was then that Eldridge began to understand more about what had been happening, how God had been leading him each step up to that point. Eldridge began to sense the difference between thought and prayer, and actually began to pray. "And from that time on, I had a deepening awareness of my surrender to Jesus Christ and of my rebirth."[12]

One change that came over Eldridge since then has been his ability to love. In the past he had quickly categorized people as friend or enemy, today he feels only one way.

"I can tell you, since that time I haven't met anyone that I don't love. Now I don't have any enemies. There may be people who don't like me. I may be their enemy; but they are not my enemy."[13]

There are many changes. From a sworn enemy of "whitey," now comes:

"I think it doesn't matter what color people are or what class they come from."[14]

From a former Communist comes:

"Now the Lord is my bridge between the hearts of all peoples and between the people and God."[15]

From a former fugitive from the law comes:

"I praise the Lord that there is nothing in the Bible that says, 'Everyone can be saved except Eldridge Cleaver.' "[16]

Eldridge accepts the changes philosophically.

"I'm just so glad I have found the Lord. Jesus completely changed my life, saved my family, brought me back home. He has given me a new life and a new song to sing. If I had known this Jesus long ago, how different my life would have been! But it's beautiful! What if it hadn't happened to me? It's better late than never!"[17]

Some of his old friends have said, "He's crazy. He made a deal. He sold out. He's an FBI agent, a CIA agent." Even the FBI—they were suspicious, Eldridge says. "They thought I had made a deal with somebody else. When I came back, everybody thought I had made a deal with somebody. I'm telling you, the police thought I had made a deal with the other police. Everybody was asking, 'Did you make a deal?' I said, 'I made a deal with Jesus!' "

During an interview on Dr. Robert Schuller's "Hour of Power," Cleaver was asked, "Eldridge, do you feel the presence of Christ in your life?"

He shot back, "Daily! And it's a breath-taking experience that's going so fast I can hardly keep up with it. I used to be embarrassed to pray with others—even with those who sincerely wanted to know that I had given my life to the Lord. But now when the prayer doors open, I just walk through. I don't hesitate—I'm not ashamed. I can even say 'Hallelujah!' It's just beautiful!"

"For He will deliver the needy when he cries for help, the afflicted also, and him who has no helper. He will have compassion . . . He will rescue their life from oppression and violence; and their blood will be precious in his sight."

— Psalm 72

111

Eldridge Cleaver, Newsmaker

BABYLON AND BEYOND
Chapter 13

"And what I advocate is the total, unequivocal destruction of capitalism. . . ."

— Cleaver, 1969

The most dramatic evidence of Cleaver's political conversion is found when you review statements he made earlier and compare them with his recent quotations.

When Cleaver was asked some years ago whether he considered the term *Babylon* to be pertinent to our times, he responded, "It's an analogue. The United States of America is described in Revelation. I'm not being a prophet. I'm just saying that I dig that. . . . Of all the symbols that I've ever run across to indicate a decadent society, I find the term Babylon, which I take from Revelation in the Bible, to be the most touching. That's how they describe Babylon—as a decadent society."[1]

"And another angel, a second one, followed, saying, 'Fallen, fallen is Babylon the Great, she who has made all the nations drink of the wine of the passion of her immorality'."

In an interview with journalist Stefan Aust at the Pan African Festival, Cleaver said, "I recognize that the United States government is the number one enemy of mankind. . . ."

During those years Cleaver made no attempt to mask his bitterness over what he felt to be a plastic Bill of Rights. The same America that stood against tyranny abroad allowed southern tyrants to enslave thousands of black human beings within her own bowels.

He repeatedly called attention to what he visualized as two contradictory images of America. On the one hand, the belief that all men are created equal and on the other, the black treatment in American history.

"The moment the blacks were let into the white world—let out of the voiceless and faceless cages of their ghettos, singing, dancing, writing, and orating their image of America and of Americans—the white world was suddenly challenged to match its practice to its preaching."[2]

He continued, "For all these years whites have been taught to believe in the myth they preached, while Negroes have had to face the bitter reality of what America practiced. . . . We force it underground, out of a perverse national modesty that reveals us as a nation of peep-freaks who prefer the bikini to the naked body. The white lie to the black truth."[3]

In conclusion, Cleaver gives vent to blacks' bitterness by declaring, "We don't care about preserving the dignity of a country that has no regard for ours. We don't give a damn about any embarrassments we may cause the United States on an international level."[4] So much for national modesty. . . .

In those years past, Cleaver evidently felt it incumbent upon himself to fill the long-vacant role of America's dirty-laundryman. He handled this position with a special bite, "The American way of life is a fossil of history . . . in a land where God is dead and the Constitution has been in a coma for 180 years."[5]

Cleaver was suggesting that the only group with potential of righting the ship of state was the blacks: "What the Negro now needs and consciously seeks is political and economic power."[6] Until that moment arrives let it be known that, "It's no secret that in America the blacks are in total rebellion against the system . . . they don't like the way America is run, from top to bottom."[7]

America, according to the old Cleaver, was a land of many people: "All with equal rights but unequal possessions. It is a land where . . . everything is owned. Everything

114

is held as private property. Someone has a brand on everything. . . . Until recently, the blacks themselves were counted as part of somebody's private property."[8]

Cleaver, when reminded that monumental strides had been taken across the land in favor of civil rights, replied, "I can only answer with what Malcolm X said, 'If you've had a knife in my back for 400 years, am I supposed to thank you for pulling it out?' "[9]

Particularly in recent years dialogue focusing on the "root of evil" has escalated. Perhaps it is a result of our own pride when cajoled into discussions concerning equality by minorities, socialists or criminals that we find it unthinkable to question their motives. Is it possible that once the median point on the totem pole is reached that their preoccupation with attainment will diminish to the extent that they are satisfied?

If money or possessions really are the root of all evil, then is it merely an irony that those adamant crusaders for unilateral parity from Moscow to Yugoslavia to Cuba are themselves the biggest capitalists of all? It was revealing when Cleaver declared that "blacks are in no position to respect or help maintain the institution of private property, what they want is to figure out a way to get some of that property for themselves."[10]

Wherever hurt, broken and bitter people are to be found, it is never long before old Karl Marx will find them and peddle his own distinctive formulas. Eldridge Cleaver, as he paced back and forth within the confines of his prison cell, was a choice target. Soon he wrote, "Everybody seemed to find it necessary to attack and condemn Karl Marx. . . . I sought out his books. . . . I was able to see in him a thoroughgoing critique and condemnation for capitalism. It was like taking medicine for me to find that, indeed, American capitalism deserved all the hatred and contempt that I felt for it in my heart."[11]

Cleaver's prison years were formative years. He continued to pour through the revolutionary writings of Marx,

115

Castro, Nechayev, Guevara, Bakunin and Mao attempting to become "an American Lenin."[12]

He began to emulate Lenin, the man Churchill had appropriately dubbed the Great Repudiator. "It became clear that it was possible for me to take the initiative. . . . I could unilaterally—whether anyone agreed with me or not—repudiate all allegiances, morals and values."[13]

While Cleaver still wasn't saying anything that hadn't been voiced before, his revolutionary rhetoric carried a new kind of bite. "This is what I'm dedicated to . . . to fight a revolutionary struggle for the violent overthrow of the United States government and the total destruction of the racist, capitalist, imperialist, neo-colonialist power structure. . . . What I advocate is the total, unequivocal destruction of capitalism and in its place a socialist system that would be compatible with the spirit of the American people. . . . There is no need for anyone to be talking about a war on poverty . . . what we need in America is a war on the rich. . . . Ideologically our hope indicates a socialist America, a communist America."[14]

Cleaver, although he didn't support the mellow methods of Martin Luther King, perhaps spotted a revolutionary springboard in his assassination. Throughout the United States the murder provided opportunity for a volcanic black rage to erupt, leaving smoldering ruins in its wake.

Cleaver in the midst of a Stanford speech, shouted, "The bullet that killed Martin Luther King murdered nonviolence, and left the bullet and the echo of the bullet here in Babylon for us to deal with." With fresh ammunition to unleash against the structure and with a new intensity in his breast, Cleaver began to vibrate sympathetically to black America's response to unavenged tyranny.

Later, after passage of yet more time and blood, Cleaver found himself discussing the American situation from the remote vantage point of Algiers: "I consider that my battlefront, the battlefront where I can make the best contribution . . . is in Babylon. This is where I want to fight! This is where I want to die. . . . Everyone has life, and in store for everyone is death—and I don't believe that there is any heaven involved. . . . If there is going to be any heaven it's going to have to be right here on earth."[15]

Cleaver, whether you agreed with his political views or not, had a laser-like insight as he reviewed Babylon and beyond. He wrote, "It is not an overstatement to say that the destiny of the entire human race depends on the outcome of what is going on in America today. This is a staggering reality to the rest of the world; they must feel like passengers in a supersonic jetliner who are forced to watch helplessly while a passel of drunks, hypes, freaks, and madmen fight for the controls and the pilot's seat. Whether America decisively moves to the right or to the left is the fundamental political problem in the world today."[16]

Cleaver expressed his views, as well, on the "Big Three" world powers. "The present persistent efforts of the U.S. to woo the Soviet Union into an alliance against China, spells *DANGER* to all the peoples of the world who have been victims of white supremacy. If this sweethearting proves successful . . . and if the U.S. is able to unleash its armed might against the rising non-white giant of China. . . . If the U.S. is successful in these areas, then it will be the black man's turn again to face the lyncher and burner of the world: and face him alone."[17]

When Cleaver left the United States after jumping bail he went first to Cuba, looking for "proletarian solidarity." This was to be the first of a number of about-the-world visits that would produce a wiser, more cautious and, ironically, a more patriotic Cleaver.

Eldridge's Political Watershed

Cleaver's stay in Cuba was brief and unpleasant. He described his feelings shortly after his return to the U.S. "It comes as a shock to you, when you think that everyone is happy under Castro's socialism, to find out how resentful they are of the economic shortages and of the contrast in the obvious privileges that party members have as opposed to regular people. There are special brigades of people who

117

run around catching the dissenters. My security man had three machine guns that he used to leave at my house. At any time of the day or night, he might run in, grab one, and run out again.

"The main point is that the people have no machinery by which to bring their will to bear upon the decision-making process. It was a sad discovery, but I found it to be so, not just in Cuba, but in all countries we traveled in, which have similar dictatorial governments. The leaders are out for themselves, not for the people. The party will destroy you at the drop of a hat."[18]

"And on the side of their oppressors was power, but they had no one to comfort them."

Columnist William F. Buckley notes, "When Cleaver was strutting about the United States denouncing it, he was never without friends, supporters and a gallery. Now that he is back sharing his experiences about that totalitarian world which he had thought of as free, he is greeted with sullenness by many student bodies and with forthright hostility by students who cannot bear to hear the former leader of the Black Panthers praise American institutions, and denounce the totalitarian ways of much of the third world. At Northwestern, he was booed when he criticized Castro's Cuba—by students who never lived in Castro's Cuba."[19]

Surprisingly, Cleaver observed, "You will find black people have more freedom in South Africa or in Rhodesia than they do in Uganda."[20] While still in Algeria he attended the Pan African Cultural Festival, as well as the International Congress of Communist Journalists. He also assembled with a group in 1971 calling itself the U.S. People's Anti-Imperialist Delegation. They enjoyed red-carpet treatment while visiting North Korea, China, and North Vietnam.

During this time of increasing disillusionment with totalitarian governments, Cleaver began to sense the brutal tug-of-war between Russia and China. "The Russians and Chinese were always vying with each other for the allegiance of everybody else. If you showed partiality toward the Chinese, then the Russians hated you—and vice versa. It was an open scandal that the Chinese and Russians were being very cynical toward the Vietnamese peoples' struggle. They liked to run in their newspapers how much they were helping liberation movements, but when you actually talked with these people, you found they drive really hard bargains. They don't even trust themselves. There is no room for this stuff about 'international brotherhood and solidarity.' After the bill is paid, you can chant those phrases; but until it's paid, it's like a confrontation."[21]

While moving throughout the communist and third world, Cleaver once heard Arabs suggest a policy of killing Americans on sight (which he denounced), and later a Soviet general and a Chinese marshal toasting the destruction of the United States. He said, "The communists were constantly carrying on planning of surprise attacks."[22] Their philosophy has long been to liberate the so-called third world countries isolating the Americans, while at the same time pushing for moral degeneration and revolution from within.

Since his conversion, Cleaver has warned, "We are living in a very dangerous international situation. The whole concept of democratic institutions is under attack, by very powerful forces that have every intention of eliminating democratic procedures, because these procedures pose a constant threat to their own authoritarian regimes. Now the Sakharovs and the Solzhenitsyns are trying to communicate to the Western world a very complicated reality: That inside the socialist countries there are people who have lived and suffered under their dictatorial regimes, and who now want democratic institutions and procedures. It's a very dangerous problem because, in order to keep the lid on it, the rules of these countries have to have a foreign devil, and that is US.[23]

119

"They are able to maintain their mobilization and every stringent control by focusing on the need to confront the United States of America. We have to be careful in safeguarding our institutions and our liberties, and in carrying on our arguments and our disagreements in a more sophisticated manner . . . we cannot afford the luxury of the kind of wild housecleaning that we have attempted in the past; that just rocks the boat until it starts to go under."[24]

That is a fascinating statement coming from a fellow who for so long didn't "give a damn" about the American establishment. Could such a metamorphosis have taken place if Cleaver had been in a jail? Perhaps his status as a fugitive was not just an odyssey but destiny. "Seeing some of their dirty laundry . . . helped to take the scales off my eyes. I am interested in resolving any differences that can be resolved with people on the right. One of the things I agree with them about is the need for a guaranteed defense. The Russians are dangerous. We cannot fall into a slumber that assumes there can be no more Pearl Harbors."[25]

If anyone knows about the malevolent intentions of the communist countries, it would certainly be their former comrade, Cleaver. But Eldridge isn't the only person now warning about these very real dangers.

General Alexander Haig, commander of NATO forces, has just said, "The Soviet Union is building up its military might and threatens the security of the Western nations. The Soviet military force has been transformed to one of global dimensions capable of supporting an imperialistic phase in their foreign policy. The buildup is not the result of a sudden Soviet decision, rather, the threat confronting us now is the product of sustained and determined Soviet defense spending, dating back at least to the Cuban missile crisis."[26]

Let Cleaver himself speak:

"Some people here are talking about Fidel Castro as some revolutionary god. Many of the Cuban people call him 'a big fat pig.' The left has to disabuse themselves of some of their political icons. I'm now glad to be able to give people on the far left a few nightmares—last time it was people on the right."[27]

Many of Cleaver's recent statements seem amazing when one considers that they come from a man who has spent much of his life in prison and much of it hating and denouncing the CIA, FBI, and police as "pigs." When queried on NBC'S *Meet the Press* about his present view of law enforcement procedures, Cleaver thoughtfully pondered:

"Well, I do dislike the illegal activities carried out by various law enforcement agencies, or security agencies, but I am also aware that other countries do the same thing. And really, when you compare our prison system or our police agencies, or the FBI or the CIA, I think they stack up very favorably with some of the others. I have unfortunately checked it out myself."

So it was possible for the new Eldridge Cleaver, having obtained an invaluable education abroad, to state, "I'd rather be in jail in America than free anywhere else."[28]

During his recent NBC *Meet the Press* interview Eldridge was asked, "What is the difference in the form of dictatorship you found there (communist and third world countries) as opposed to the kind you charged existed here in the U.S.A. in the 1960s?"

He replied, "I think there is a great difference. In the first place, I think the United States cannot be accurately described as a dictatorship. If I said that in the past, I think I would be guilty of an excessive use of language."

Eldridge now feels the Black Panthers were "a little naive" in their approach. "I think we were excessive in some of our language. I think we scared a lot of people . . . if I had it to do all over again, I would do it differently."[29]

Eldridge continued, "In the past, the question was raised as to whether or not blacks were going to be a part of America . . . I think that question has been resolved. We are inside the system, and I feel that the No. 1 objective for black Americans is to recognize that they have the same equal rights under the Constitution as Rockefeller, even if we have no blue-chip stocks. But our membership in the United States is the supreme blue-chip stock, and the one we have to exercise.

"I believe that every American, regardless of his politics, has a duty to reexamine his beliefs. This is particularly true of those active at both extremes of the political spectrum. Those of us who developed a psychology of opposition must take a pause and sum up our experiences. We must recognize that in a sense we are playing a brand new ballgame. The slogans of yesterday will not get us through the tasks at hand. . . .

"With all of its faults, the American political system is the freest and the most democratic in the world. The system needs to be improved, with democracy spread to all areas of life, particularly the economic. All of these changes must be conducted through our established institutions, and the people with grievances must find political methods for obtaining redress.

"I think that my generation has been more critical than most. . . . At the end of the critical process, we should arrive at some conclusions. We should have discovered which values are worth conserving. It is the beginning of another fight—the fight to defend those values from the blind excesses. . . . It is my hope to make a positive contribution in this regard."[30]

Well, there you have it. The prodigal son has returned! I believe that America's response to Eldridge Cleaver ought not be any less than WELCOME HOME!

122

Eldridge Cleaver voted for the first time in 1976. Cleavers emerge from polling place.

SOUL TALK
Chapter 14

After first meeting Eldridge and Kathleen on the day he was a guest on my television show, I asked if they had yet met Pat and Shirley Boone. It turned out they hadn't, and we agreed their meeting one another should be worked out. But since both Pat Boone and Eldridge were on tight schedules, it was two months later when their first meeting at the Boones' Beverly Hills home finally came about.

Pat was immediately off again, to Canada this time, keeping his schedule of public concerts. We finally caught up with him by telephone in Toronto and asked what had happened when they got together. He said he would write me as it would take too long to tell on the phone. Here is a portion of Pat's letter:

"It was one of the most unforgettable nights of my whole life. Eldridge Cleaver came to dinner!

"My mind and emotions were doing flip-flops. Just a very few years earlier, I had threatened to take my daughter, Debby, out of the girls' school she was attending because the teacher had assigned Cleaver's *Soul on Ice* for the girls to read! I had gone over to the school, had a long meeting with the teacher, and let him know in no uncertain terms that I felt he was dead-wrong to assign a book like this for 16-year-old girls to read!

"He stuck to his guns, though, and insisted that a number of them were already buying this book on their own and reading it anyway; and he felt it would be better to go ahead and discuss this kind of subject matter in a classroom situation. I reminded him there were many things that teenage girls get involved in on their own time that don't belong in classrooms as assignments to be graded.

"We seemed to be getting no place, so I told him that I

125

would not allow Debby to read Cleaver's book; and, unless he gave her an alternate assignment, I would enroll her someplace else. When the teacher asked her, Debby hesitantly agreed with me that she really didn't want to be exposed to that kind of militant, vulgar, and antisocial thought. She had enough other things to cope with. As it turned out, the teacher dropped that assignment for her and Debby was allowed to give a report on something else.

"And now here were Eldridge and his wife, Kathleen, joining us around our dinner table—and we were praying!

"But just before we bowed our heads, he had let us know that he too was going through a real culture shock. He told us how, years before, he and other young black kids had driven through Beverly Hills, looking at the houses and sizing them up for possible future robberies. Eldridge felt certain that the old Cleaver had cased our house. And now it was a mind-wrenching experience to be *in* that very house, by invitation.

"It was a long and super evening. In the hours that passed, the Cleavers and our family shared experiences and came to know each other pretty well. We were moved to tears as we heard how the Lord had met Eldridge and brought him back to the United States to accept responsibility for certain past actions and to seek God's new direction for his life.

"We learned something more of the trauma for him to voluntarily walk back into prison where he knew he could die. Eldridge's grasp of the Word and sense of God's hand on their new life was deeply stirring. They, like Shirley and me, have a lot of growing to do and many tests and challenges (and perhaps disappointments) ahead; but they have embarked and are not planning to look back, God being their help.

"The dominant message of the gospel is its 'good news' that we don't, any of us, have to stay as we are; that we can be changed and transformed into something better and more beautiful.

"Wherever He went in His earthly ministry, Jesus met

126

people like Eldridge and me—and He changed them! After the new birth that He taught us about, there comes a lifelong period of growth and development and maturing and then passing it on.

"I am just grateful Jesus is still open for business and meeting the needs of people like me.

In Him,
Pat Boone"

Eldridge and Kathleen with Pat and Shirley Boone

Chapter 15

The old Cleaver once raged, ". . . pigs of the cloth. I don't care if they say a eulogy over me or not. They can spit on me and flush me down the toilet when I'm gone. I don't need their holy water. I don't need their prayers."[1] Along the same atheistic vein he wrote, "While all this was going on, our group was espousing atheism . . . our atheism was pragmatic. I had come to believe that there is no God; if there is, men do not know anything about him. Therefore, all religions were phoney. . . ."[2]

But that Cleaver is gone and what a change!

Ken Overstreet, of Youth for Christ, shared part of a letter Eldridge wrote to him last year. "Since I turned to Jesus, so many fantastically good things have been happening to me that each day seems to bring new miracles. Everything seems to be exhilarating on the spiritual, and I find myself growing stronger and stronger in the faith. I actually recall feeling like a little babe in Christ. Now I feel myself an infant, a little more developed, a little stronger than a babe, but definitely still a little child, but growing stronger."[3]

Through a unique chain of events, though his outward appearance is the same, Eldridge is a different person—a man recycled by God. The Word says after spiritual rebirth we become "a new creation." No wonder he sounds new—HE IS NEW! But you simply can't resist questioning Eldridge about these differences. And so, from recent interviews let's get better acquainted with this new believer through an edited composite of recent interviews and lectures:

QUESTION: For years you were a zealous God-denying

Marxist, subscribing to its definition of religion as "the opiate of the people and part of the apparatus of oppression." With that in mind, tell us how you interpreted your Jesus in the moon experience.

ELDRIDGE: "I have to paint you a context in which that took place because this was at the end of seven years." *(He tells how he went from Cuba to Algeria and finally arrived with political asylum in France.)* "I found myself at the end of my rope, you might say. I had already, before the vision, seen through the philosophy of Marxist-Leninism. I had seen the practices of the communist countries. I had seen the life of the people under those regimes, and I had reached the point where I had seen through that philosophy and had rejected it."[4]

(Eldridge then explains how he felt stranded in France, with no way to turn, no way to end his man-without-a-country situation. He described his commuting between his family in Paris and his books and manuscripts in his Mediterranean apartment, his feeling of despair, and finally, his depression.)

ELDRIDGE (continuing): "One night, in this very depressed state of mind, I found myself sitting on my 12th-story balcony under this clear Mediterranean sky with all of the stars and a very full moon—not really totally full; there were shadows on the moon. I was just sitting there alone, looking up at the moon and brooding about all these problems.

"The shadows on the moon suddenly formed into a face. It was my face! I saw myself in the moon. I said, 'Maybe this is some premonition of death.' It frightened me. I had a beard in this image that I saw. There was a succession of mostly bearded men. . . . I saw Fidel Castro and I saw Karl Marx with all of his hair. It was like someone had a slide machine, projecting on the moon. Then there was Mao Tse-tung, without a beard. Then all of a sudden there was one final face—the face of Jesus Christ! Now this really was the last straw. I didn't hear any voices. It really upset me because I am not one who had gone around thinking about Jesus. I started crying."[5]

QUESTION: Did you think you were losing your mind, or that this was some significant vision? Could you identify it?

ELDRIDGE: "I was afraid I was coming unglued. I didn't know what to think! I was just overwhelmed. And I started crying then, uncontrollably. Now, I wasn't the one to cry. I fell down on my knees and said parts of the Lord's prayer and the 23rd Psalm again and again which I—"[6]

QUESTION: Had you memorized these when you were a child? Is that why they came back to you at that time?

ELDRIDGE: "I had almost forgotten it since a boy; but also among the books on my shelf inside my apartment, I had the Bible which we kept through my travels. I went and found that Bible and began to read . . . the 23rd Psalm again. After I don't know how long, I got up and went inside. I went to sleep. For years my sleep had been very troubled. My sleep had always been so broken. And I can't really say that I had even been sleeping very much at nights. But after that experience, I had the most peaceful sleep that I had ever had."[7]

(The next day Eldridge awoke in a cheerful spirit. No depression. He did not dwell much that day on his experience of seeing Jesus. He really did not know what to make of it. What he did have on his mind was going home. Still. . . .)

ELDRIDGE (continuing): "It was a precious moment that I guard and I cherish because now, in retrospect, I can see that that was my real confrontation with Jesus Christ and the beginning of my life turning around."[8]

QUESTION: It seems pretty clear, Eldridge, that of all

131

those figures in the moon, just that one stuck out for you. The one that began to burn in your head was the figure of Jesus. It started with your own image and then a parade of your former communist heroes. After Jesus looked at you, did everything seem to melt? Did you have any feeling of a contact with God?

ELDRIDGE: "It was a focus on God, a focus on Jesus— because it was a rejection of the others. And I could see that I was rejecting them. These were the false gods that I had been through and I was rejecting them. Yes, I was seeing that."[9]

QUESTION: Now you were really in a critical position. Suddenly the world you had given your life to—the cause you believed was the answer—the world in which you had become a leader, suddenly to see that old world crumbling must have been shattering. But in this moment of deepest despair, God sent you His Son in a vision.

ELDRIDGE: "Yes, but I didn't understand what all this meant for many months."[10]

QUESTION: You have been quoted as saying that Communists are united by hate and Christians are united by love.

ELDRIDGE: "Human beings are defined as members of one class or the other. The relationship between those two classes is defined by the Manifesto as one of strife, war and conflict. The Communists' basic definition of every person is one at war with his fellow man. Hate and struggle, not peace and love."[11]
(Nor can one resist testing him with religious questions, especially me.)

QUESTION: Now after your encounter with Jesus, what do you think of the Bible? Many say it is a book of poetry,

132

folklore and history. What do you believe the Bible to be?

ELDRIDGE: "I believe that Book to be God's message and guidance to mankind."[12]

QUESTION: Do you actually believe it is still relevant here in the 20th century? It was written thousands of years ago. How can such a book be practical and relevant in this modern day?

ELDRIDGE: "I can just tell you from my own personal experience—a very recent experience—that the Bible is both practical and alive in my life. I have taken it as the guide for the rest of my life; and if this present moment is relevant, the Bible is absolutely relevant."[13]

QUESTION: Eldridge, I would like to ask you who you believe Jesus Christ was—or is?

ELDRIDGE: "I base my opinion on what is taught in the Bible. The Bible teaches us that Jesus is God manifested to us in flesh. And Jesus is the Son of God sent to mankind here on earth. And Jesus is the Saviour of those who believe on Him. I do not quarrel with that definition. When I placed my faith, Jesus entered my life. I have had the personal experience of being picked up and salvaged by Jesus, so now I take Jesus as my personal Saviour—as the Son of God, sent to mankind for salvation of the world."[14]

QUESTION: But you know Jesus was accused and sentenced—like you have experienced. Yet He was executed 1900 years ago and was buried. How could He have any meaningful relationship to us now, since He was executed?

ELDRIDGE: "He was executed, in a manner of speaking, but He then arose from the dead; and He has sent down through the centuries and through the dark hours His life, His testimony and His witness."[15]

(Eldridge speaks earnestly as he relates how, through this life and through this witness, people have had access to salvation so that—although it was 1900 years ago—it is utterly relevant at this moment . . . indeed the living Bible.

And one cannot help but ask questions about Kathleen's reaction to this change.)

QUESTION: How did you tell Kathleen about this change?

ELDRIDGE: "I waited a few days to try and sort it out. The two of us were sitting on the bed in Paris. Well, in a sort of roundabout way, I talked to her about the moon—but not directly. I knew what she would say *(He paused, then chuckled.)* . . . that I was loony."[16]

QUESTION: Shortly after your return home, there were reports that Kathleen said that you really hadn't received Jesus as your Lord.

ELDRIDGE: "There are two explanations. Both my attorney (at the time) and Kathleen were concerned that news leaking about my finding Christ might dry up some financial resources needed for my legal expenses. Secondly, she didn't feel comfortable at first dealing with this new aspect of my life. Now we both can freely talk about it."[17]

(Eldridge explains how Kathleen was right, as some of those funds did dry up. Then his face lights up as he tells how new friends are beginning to help.)

QUESTION: Is Kathleen a Christian now? How does she feel about the Bible?

ELDRIDGE: "Kathleen and I are one. And we've been together now for seven years. We're united in wedlock and we've passed on the breath of life to our two children; and we are together. I'll just tell you that Kathleen is a Christian. *(He describes how, in October 1976, he and*

134

Kathleen were baptized in the Campus Crusade pool.)
"We've never been more happy."[18]

QUESTION: Have you noticed any changes in your relations with others since your spiritual encounter?

ELDRIDGE: "Yes, there used to be a gulf, a hostility toward some groups and people. But now it's like everybody is my brother and sister. The bridge between us is Jesus—and God—and I'm thankful for these new friends."

(No more questions).

Eldridge and Kathleen on television set with host, George Otis

Maceo, Eldridge, Thelma (Eldridge's mother), Kathleen and Joju.

SUSPENDED BETWEEN TWO WORLDS
Chapter 16

"My life has turned 180 degrees; I would call it a conversion experience . . . I view that night as my conversion experience because I was not the same after it as I was before."[1]

Still many people are wondering whether that's for real. Some worry it may just be a clever trick of the communists; sending Cleaver back to infiltrate the ranks of their archenemies—the Christians and right-wingers.

Some are asking whether his new religion and politics weren't a deliberate affectation to get himself back into the country and off the hook for his part in the shootout and his subsequent bail jumping. Another school is asking whether the big 6 foot, 2 inch, 220-pound black is just going through another one of his frequent mutations.

This latter school of Cleaver-watchers believe their cynicism is warranted because of his past history. They point out that Cleaver has always been in a state of flux: from the little Baptist Sunday Schooler to the East L.A. petty criminal and school dropout; soon followed by a quick baptism in the Roman Catholic Church. Later in prison these phases speeded up even more: Plato and the philosophers; Tom Paine, Emerson and Thoreau; Rosicrucianism; the Black Muslim religion; socialism. Finally, all this Cleaver searching led to his big, 18-year love affair with Marxism.

Not too surprisingly they're mumbling, "I wonder what Cleaver will next turn to after he tires of this Jesus trip? And how can such a bitter revolutionary turn so quickly to being an apostle of Christianity?"

Anyway, Eldridge Cleaver was free, at least for a while. And what a paradox! It wasn't the Panthers, the communists, the ACLU, or his past friends from the left who made his temporary freedom possible. Speaking slowly and with a soft voice the 41-year-old Eldridge Cleaver told, on August 13, 1976, how he was freed on a $100,000 bail bond, largely because of collateral supplied by a wealthy Christian businessman. By a formerly hated WASP (White Anglo-Saxon Protestant)! Rescued by a man who embodied five characteristics which had repulsed Cleaver for so many years. His new bail-bond angel was not only rich, white, a political conservative and from the business world but also—a fervent Christian! This real-life hero was Arthur DeMoss, founder of the Pennsylvania-based National Liberty Corporation.

DeMoss had visited Eldridge in jail, reviewing Scriptures with him. The insurance executive's spiritual discernment had "clicked" after face-to-face meetings with the former fugitive. The Bible says, in effect, we aren't just to say, "God bless, I'll be praying for you," but to help and visit those in need. Yes, help toward their practical needs. Arthur DeMoss followed these scriptural guidelines to the limit. Soon he put up $50 thousand of his own personal savings as collateral to bail out his new friend, fully conscious that Cleaver had jumped the last bail. This came not only as a surprise to Eldridge, but as another thundering testimony of God's hand in his life during that critical era of transition from his old world to the new. (The slightly built DeMoss, though head of a major corporation, finds great satisfaction slipping off to rural Mexico to preach the gospel and help the poor.) Eldridge, since his bail freedom, has shared time and prayer with Billy Graham, Pat Matrisciana, Chuck Colson, Pat Boone, and other mature Christians.

Even so, the questions linger on in some Christian circles. At one stage Eldridge was quoted as being furious at one jail chaplain's tattling about his conversion and the story's implication that it had occurred suddenly. Eldridge had angrily insisted the change in his life had been brought about through a long series of processes and experiences.

However, several weeks after the burst of anger, he sheepishly admitted that the chaplain's breaking of the story had been a blessing after all.

In Russ Chandler's *Los Angeles Times* article, "Cleaver's New Direction and Goal," Eldridge described the mystical night on the balcony as his turning point, "I view this night as my conversion experience because I was not the same after it as before."

In his trial Eldridge is facing three counts each of attempted murder and assaulting the police. But massive evidence in both word and deed indicate he has rejected a 1968 oath, supposedly made in San Francisco, that he would "bring an evil, arrogant, crazy American system crashing down!" Since coming home, he has cried out to all who would listen that he now knows the communist ideology is spiritually bankrupt and that he began to realize "man cannot live by bread alone."

Eldridge Cleaver now seems most intent in persuading others about his new ideology through lectures and writing. Newly armed with the Sword of the Spirit he moves to campus, church, civic auditorium, to television talk-shows, proclaiming Eldridge's ultimate discovery—salvation through Christ.

In retrospection, he admits that Bible teaching and religious concepts learned while he was a boy rose up to face him throughout the radical years. More and more, the questions he had to decide were not about politics or tactics but about moral values. He once said, "I felt poorly equipped to deal with these problems of right and wrong . . . I had to revert back to those religious principles to resolve the questions. At times, it troubled me, drawing on the opium of the masses—but I couldn't shake off the power in the Golden Rule. Of course, seeing some of their dirty laundry . . . helped to take the scales off my eyes . . . Communism's denial of the human soul, of the existence of anything other than material made me feel threatened. . . ."[2]

One of Cleaver's former heroes, because of his writing power, was Thomas Paine, who energized the American

Revolution. It isn't unreasonable to foresee that Eldridge's pen and tongue may prove to be even mightier in our modern-day spiritual revolution than Paine's in his.

The project which is now "most dear" to Eldridge is a work of his pen. It will be the sequel to his biggest book and just as *Soul on Ice* was an expression of philosophies and theory of his former life, so its sequel, *Soul on Fire,* to be published by Word, will be an updating of his new views. What a book that will be! It will run richly with many things only he is privileged to know—and about which only Eldridge Cleaver can write.

But Eldridge isn't just yaking, writing, and racing around. It's as if he's turned his transmitter way down and his receiver way up. During a recent noon hour gospel rally, headed by evangelist Leon Ralph, Eldridge was standing in the crowd. It took place on the north lawn of the Sacramento state Capitol. A reporter spotted the international figure standing there on the fringe holding his suit coat. When the reporter rushed up, Cleaver waved him back to avoid distracting attention from the evangelist. The reporter asked him what he was doing there.

Eldridge replied, "I'm here for what you should be doing—listening."[3] And that's what he is doing a lot of these days. He's in such demand he could be speaking seven times a day, seven days of the week, but recognizes the importance of "taking in."

These days Eldridge Cleaver is listening to Bible teaching on cassettes. He is reading and submitting to lots of personal counseling. This, too, is reminiscent of the apostle Paul of old, who, for several years threw his own busy life into neutral, to re-learn after his own Damascus Road conversion.

140

Cleaver comes home with his shocking story of conversion

Chapter 17

That Eldridge is controversial all right! People on both sides of the fence are still trying to get a fix on him—and with only partial success. Some conservatives have jumped the gun and have him joining the Birch Society. At the same time, a few leftist groups are working on him, not convinced their old hero has stood them up.

In a recent *People* magazine interview he was asked, "Some of your old friends denounce you as a right-winger. How much have your politics changed?" Eldridge shot back, "I have the same criticism of this country. I think my criticisms are even more to the point, more surgical. But I am interested in resolving any differences that can be resolved with people on the right. . . . The Russians are dangerous. . . . We cannot fall into a slumber that assumes there can be no more Pearl Harbors."

Later in the interview, "How can you account for all this mellowing toward the establishment figures?" Eldridge answered, "I used to have the attitude that people were out to do me in on a physical level. That is why I used to relate to guns a lot. But I tell you, ever since that strange experience, I haven't met a person I didn't like. I haven't. I might be some kind of failure. Maybe some tubes and fuses were blown."

At the close of the interview, "And what about your future? Are you going to undertake some sort of Christian activist crusade?" Eldridge replied, "I have no plans like that. I picture myself as a writer and a speaker and that is what I will do. If that constitutes a crusade. . . ."[1]

Again we catch sparks from the flashing pen of William F. Buckley. In his column titled, "Cleaver's Out of Fashion," he wrote, "As a young man, Cleaver began as a desperado of sorts. . . . He then consecrated his violence to the ideals of Marxist revolution. He wrote a searing book of hatred called *Soul on Ice.* . . . All that Eldridge Cleaver put behind him when he arrived back in the United States. And he was to face the bitterest experience of all. When Cleaver was strutting about the United States denouncing it, he was never without friends, supporters, and a gallery. Now that he is back sharing his experiences in that totalitarian world . . . he is greeted with sullenness by many student bodies and with forthright hostility by students who cannot bear to hear the former leader of the Black Panthers praise American institutions and denounce the totalitarian ways of much of the third world."[2]

In so many ways Eldridge is still a man without a country. Like Saul who was caught in the cross fire between his former Pharisee friends and new Christian friends, Eldridge often walks in that same no-man's-land. Often catching a measure of suspicion and damnation from both sides—suspended between two worlds.

But Eldridge is neither a coward nor a fool. Can you imagine the courage needed to vacate his longtime throne as Heavyweight Champion fighting against America, democracy, and God? And don't ever think that before the change he didn't foresee the consequences.

The old Cleaver was human enough to thrive in the spotlight as Super Critic, knowing full well how much easier it is to hold the limelight as a "hater" than as a defender. He knew before he ever switched sides that, ever-after, he would face not only the wrath but perhaps the gun of his old friends.

And sure enough, since back, he has heard both the saber rattling and the whistle of their verbal arrows. T.D. Altman, director of an urban research project at the University of California, was interviewing him when Eldridge groaned.

"If you think it is easy to revise your views in public, to have your old friends call you a traitor, your old enemies try to use you, just try it yourself."[3]

Displaying sheer guts, he has walked onto podia on one campus after another, boldly sharing his new discoveries while taking the harassment from a few. Victories resulting from Eldridge's new campus thunder have so unnerved the lefties that some are now saturating the campuses he's headed for with anti-Cleaver propaganda.

One "for instance" was a bulletin put out over the signature of The Revolutionary Student Brigade titled *"Eldridge (Sold Out) Cleaver: Comes Home to Slander People's Struggle."* It reads in part, "Less than a year ago Cleaver crawled back from exile a traitor to the struggle. . . . He says that justice can now be found in America. Well, maybe after this tour he can find 'justice.' But the murders of George Jackson, Fred Hampton, the Attica inmates, and the students at Kent and Jackson go unavenged. And the system is still trying to drag people like Hurricane Carter and Johnny Ross over the coals. . . .

"Cleaver is also peddling statements like 'the United States . . . is the freest, most democratic country in the whole world.' Coming out of a Presidential election where we were permitted to pick the capitalist front man 'of our choice' — Mr. Terrible or Mr. Worst Yet—we know just what Cleaver's idea of democracy is worth. . . . Today Cleaver is nothing more than a spokesman for the rich class that was once the target of the Black Panther Party. . . .

"While Cleaver was exiled . . . he grew increasingly alienated from the people's struggles, which range in order from the SLA-type urban guerrilla warfare in the U.S. in which a handful of revolutionaries were bringing down the imperialist system . . . just as more people were coming to recognize that fundamental change could only come through masses of people led by the multi-national working class uniting and organizing themselves to fight the capitalist system. While Cleaver was safe in Algiers, dozens of young blacks who wanted to fight oppression were slaughtered or jailed trying to carry out Cleaver's suicidal line. . . ."

The Brigade's volley from the left flank concludes,

"Poor Eldridge found countries like the Democratic Peoples Republic of Korea and the Republic of China oppressive because there was no place for his jive line or his hotpants. . . . When the pay-back comes he'll just find out what revolutionary hotpants are all about."

That is threatening rhetoric. But Eldridge is too bright and too experienced with what is really happening in the other camp. Neither pamphleteers nor hecklers know quite how to handle him. When some auditorium troublemaker lets go he is often looking for a rock to crawl under when Eldridge's responding facts level him.

Cleaver simply has too much personal knowledge about the leaders and actual conditions in the communist and socialist countries to be downed by any person mouthing half-facts. One of Eldridge's recent campus speeches was interrupted by a black foreign student's persistent attacks about the horrible repressions going on in the U.S.A.

Finally Eldridge interrupted his lecture and asked the heckler for the name of his home country. The heckling student refused his repeated requests. But Eldridge gently pressed in and drew more and more bits of information from the increasingly flustered black, who had been castigating America for its lack of freedom.

Suddenly Eldridge had extracted enough clues from him and pounced, "Son, the head of your country is President-for-life, Field Marshal Idi Amin. The capital city of your homeland is Kampala. I believe you have an airport called Entebbe.

"What was that again you were just telling us about all the repressions here in the United States?"

There was dead silence; and at the close of Eldridge's lecture the university auditorium filled with applause.

Still another fascinating confrontation is reported by T.D. Altman in a *New York Times* article, "The Rebirth of Eldridge Cleaver." It reads in part:

"A young black man was standing toward the back of the room, visibly ill-at-ease among the Tulane students. His voice was uncertain as it began, but then it released a torrent

146

of sentences that never quite ended, of ideas that never fully coalesced, of points that never got made. He ended by demanding why Cleaver no longer had anything to say to black people.

"Cleaver was as cool as if he had been asked a hostile question on 'Meet the Press.'

" 'I don't speak to black people,' he said, 'I don't speak to white people. I speak to Americans.'

"The young man forced his way from the room."[4]

In spite of such problems Eldridge is being heard on American campuses and with unprecedented results. (But don't think the hail of critical barbs is easy to take.) Like King Saul of the Old Testament Eldridge has become *ANOTHER MAN;* newly sensitized and tired of hate. He is also a proud man and the barrage of criticism from both flanks stings.

Not all Christians are as ready to put their money on Eldridge Cleaver as was Arthur DeMoss. A few are still ready to hold the coat of his stoners. There still hovers uncertainty and vacillation in some parts of the church. By the fall of 1976 the word was out about the shocking spiritual metamorphosis of Cleaver the caterpillar to Eldridge the butterfly. It was about that time High Adventure TV did the first on-camera probing of Eldridge Cleaver's spiritual views. During the course of this interview I asked point blank who he felt Jesus is; the relevance and authorship of the Bible, and so on.

Eldridge responded with positive on-target answers and I became convinced it was time for two things to be initiated:

First: To arrange for him to guest on a Christian television call-in program. Second: To arrange for him to address, for the first time, an all-faiths audience in a church setting. It seemed important to allow his spirit to be directly felt by the Christian community.

Response to our initial efforts was mixed: The first host of one of the out-of-town Christian talk shows said, in effect, "Oh no, we're not too sure about him. Not with his

147

background, we've got to wait and see whether he's real. And that may take a long time."

It was a loud "No" to a Cleaver appearance.

But that wasn't the end of it. Two months afterward Eldridge was seen and heard by the nationwide TV audiences of PTL Network, Charlotte, North Carolina, and the 700 Club, Portsmouth, Virginia.

Eldridge passed with flying colors!

Efforts to find a suitable church podium for the new Eldridge was likewise met with a measure of nervousness. One example may suffice: The sanctuary of historic Hollywood First Presbyterian was requested for the meeting. Its central location, reputation and facilities seemed ideal for Eldridge's debut. Its genial pastor, after listening to the sound track of the High Adventure program, agreed to recommend that their sanctuary be made available to host Eldridge's church premiere. Our people got busy on the phones to Christian leaders and prominent lay people.

But shortly the church's officialdom met in solemn session. An embarrassed representative stammered, "We're so sorry but the lay leadership has voted down permission to use our church for the Cleaver meeting. They don't feel we should take chances."

Now let's not fault "Hollywood Pres", for it wasn't the only church to decline the honor of welcoming a speaker they remembered as a blaspheming revolutionary.

But soon thereafter Rev. Sanders of North Hollywood Assembly prayed, then promptly rolled out the red carpet. His people thought the risks well worth taking to play host to what they suspected might become an historical gathering. A blizzard of new phone calls went out changing the meeting place. On the appointed evening the church was overflowing by the time a husky-voice Eldridge walked to the podium.

His first church meeting was replete with a bomb threat and hecklers but it ended in celebration! Eldridge, "preacher and evangelist," was received with more applause and acceptance than any Hollywood star at a premiere. It wasn't what he said or even how he said it. It was his eyes, his countenance and his bearing—all telegraphing the "goodest of the Good News."

Spiritual Warfare

This planet is accurately depicted as a battleground between God and malevolent forces arrayed against His people and His Kingdom. This fight against God is orchestrated by Satan, a very real being. He is also called the "prince of this world," and himself desires to exert dominion over men's minds.

People at times, deliberately or unknowingly, become instruments through which either good or evil is worked. Even godly people themselves can, through carelessness, be used against the purposes of God. On the other hand, even an atheist or an agnostic can at times be used by God to bring about His purposes. In real-life some players not only *can* but *do* change sides, occasionally.

We just witnessed such a role change. The new Eldridge was making himself available for the church and television to advance the Kingdom of God, but a few established Christians blocked his ministry temporarily.

Has this ever happened before?

Of course it has.

The early Christians of Paul's day also regarded him, at first, with distrust and suspicion. In his old life his name was Saul (like the *Cleaver* of old). Historic accounts tell us a lot about his former actions against Divine purposes. We read, "(Saul) yet breathing out threatenings and slaughter against the disciples of the Lord" went to the High Priest and secured the necessary papers of authority to go to Damascus and put any Christians he could find there in chains and bring them back to Jerusalem for punishment.

After his conversion being called Paul (like the new *Eldridge*), he described his former activities, "I verily thought ... that I ought to do many things contrary to the name of Jesus of Nazareth, which thing I did also in Jerusalem and many of the saints did I shut up in prison

149

having received authority from the Chief Priest; and when they were put to death I gave my voice against them. And I punished them oft in every synagogue, and compelled them to blaspheme and being exceedingly furious against them I persecuted them. . . ."

Now Eldridge might be upset when he reads how we have compared elements of his own conversion with the mighty Apostle Paul's. But these words aren't his observations—they're mine and I know of the differences in their lives as well as the heart-warming similarities.

We know from history that while Stephen, the first martyr, was being stoned to death the old Saul was not only in agreement with his stoners but personally held the coat of one of the murderers. Saul worked to make havoc of the church, acting at times like some wild man entering into homes and synagogues dragging off Christians to prison.

Later, a converted Paul wrote to his young friend, Timothy, about this era of his life when he was fighting against the purposes of God. "I was a blasphemer and a persecutor and injurious." Later Paul cried to the church in Corinth, "I am the least of the apostles—not fit to be called an apostle because I persecuted the church of God—oppressing it with cruelty and violence."

No wonder Christians were afraid of the old Saul. And not surprising that some were afraid of the old Cleaver who also ranted at Christians, the Bible and at God Himself. But something happened to both Saul and Cleaver which inspires us to know that God takes pleasure in dealing with "impossible people." There came a day when God touched each of these men with awakening visions and each was made a new creation. Upon Paul and Eldridge came God's instantaneous touch followed up by an ongoing process through the Holy Spirit.

In a letter to the Galatians, Paul shared about his own activities after conversion on the Damascus Road. Paul said he didn't immediately tell everybody about his experience. He traveled into Arabia, then on to Damascus. After three years Paul met with Peter at Joppa and Caesarea for more preparation. It was 14 long years before Paul ever got back to the city he had started out from—Jerusalem.

God had many things to say to Paul, whom He had chosen, and seemed in no hurry to thrust him into ministry. But after his re-learning years, Paul went out in the power of God and helped "turn the world upside down." Since the end of this present age seems near, there may not be as much time for Eldridge to enjoy the long tutoring Paul enjoyed.

What Saul had started (and what I trust Eldridge will help finish) was so explosive neither man nor devil could stop him!

The Jews were furious about Saul's conversion. Some were described as gnashing their teeth "lest they should kill Paul. One night the Christians had to let Paul down in a basket to escape a band of men who had come to murder him: The Jews plotted together to do away with him . . . and they were always watching the gates day and night so that they might put him to death."

The Christians didn't exactly receive Saul with open arms either. A few days after his conversion, Ananias was told to go pray for the vision-blinded convert. But he was hesitant because of Saul's fierce reputation against Christians. Ananias was filled with astonishment mingled with fear, and tried to tell the Lord what an evil man Saul had been. As if God didn't already know!

Later, when the "born again" and renamed Paul tried to make his defense before the Jews, they listened to his conversion story politely up to the point where he dared to say that God had directed him to go minister to the Gentiles. When the Jews heard that, they exploded. The Bible describes the scene: "They raised their voices and said away with such a fellow from the earth, for he shall not be allowed to live."

But at such times God always sends an encourager; in Paul's case, it was Barnabas. His name in Hebrew appropriately means "son of consolation." We read how this same

Barnabas, "took hold of him (Paul) and brought him to the apostles and described to them how he had seen the Lord. . . . "

Good for you, Barnabas! May there be many who will now rise up to help Eldridge. Christians surely haven't been quick to accept him and it was the same with Paul. "And when he had come to Jerusalem, he was trying to associate with the disciples; and they were all afraid of him."

But from about that time on, it would seem that Paul preached freely wherever God directed him to go. Paul's enemies have faded into history while he went on to be so used of God that the light of his ministry illuminates every continent to this day.

Now Eldridge has emerged from the 40 wilderness years of his former life and is likewise in preparation to shine. How much light will his new life cast in the days ahead?

A new creation

THE JUDGE OF JUDGES!
Chapter 18

"The legal system is not there for someone to save face. The legal system is there to determine innocence or guilt. And if you're found innocent, that's a victory for the court. It's not a sign of weakness. And if they find you guilty and it's a true finding, that's not a sign of weakness either. That's a sign that the courts work."

— Cleaver[1]

Having already spent half his life in reform schools, jails and prisons, there is nothing Eldridge fears more than being locked up again. Even so, resisting God is one mistake Eldridge is now determined to avoid. "I am resigned to the will of the Lord about whether I go to prison for the charges against me . . . and will try to be sensitive about how to best serve Him wherever that might be."[2]

Caging a caterpillar doesn't seem too serious—but to cage a butterfly?

You have been privileged to enormous information about Mr. Cleaver's past and present. Enough facts to make a sound judgment on his case.

Just suppose you have suddenly been appointed as a jury of one; and through your own judgment his entire future will now rest.

What will you do with this man? To what kind of a future will you consign him?

Eldridge Cleaver's Day in Court
[The judge gavels the court into session.]
The prosecuter rises to address the court:

155

"Your honor, it takes many shelves just to hold the defendant's court and police records for prior crimes of drug peddling, thievery, rape and violence. Since his youth he has been an incorrigible. For years Mr. Cleaver fought against the police and downed the nation; even threatening to level America. He gave aid and comfort to her enemies.

"The defendant schooled revolutionaries; consorted with criminals and was captured after a bloody shootout with police. He then fled the country to avoid prosecution and is an admitted bail jumper.

"Why, seven of his shootout compatriots have already been tried and each was eventually convicted.

"I say away with this troublemaker, you must protect society and put him in prison for life! The prosecution now rests."

There is a rustling as the prosecuting attorney walks back to his seat. A mixture of applause and boos fills the courtroom.

The judge brings down his gavel and warns, "We will have order in this court!"

[It is time for the summation by the defense in the case of the People versus Eldridge Cleaver.]

The defense attorney rises to address the court: "Your honor, the prosecuting attorney has given a proper summation of the People's case against my client. With your permission I shall now submit additional facts to the jury."

The judge nods, "Proceed with your defense arguments, counselor."

The lawyer slowly turns and looks straight at you, "Did you know that the late J. Edgar Hoover himself described a systematic campaign of the FBI to discredit and neutralize the activities of black organizations, like the Panthers, and their leaders? And that Mr. Cleaver was a focus of this campaign? Did you know that before the shootout in 1968, it is rumored the FBI lied to the Oakland police; telling them the Panthers had gotten machine guns? Do you realize that this report may have helped trigger the '68 tragedy?

156

"Do you recall that there is no admissible evidence Mr. Cleaver fired a gun the night of April 6. That you must take into account the nationwide conditions in America during the week of the shootout: Dr. King's assassination, black grief, riots and burning across the country. Don't forget my client's efforts to cool the ghetto hotheads.

"And I object, your honor, to my colleague's recital of the crimes of the defendant's youth. He already paid for these with nearly half his years in prison. We must exclusively address ourselves to the outstanding shootout and bail jumping issues."

Then further, "Hasn't Mr. Cleaver already paid enough for any alleged violations connected with his role in the shootout through his seven painful exile years, plus his many months served in prison since his return? Are we to give this man no consideration for his voluntary surrender?

"In my arguments in his behalf I must now ask you to take into account this fundamental question:

"Are we trying the right man?"

[The courtroom explodes with stomping, shouts, boos, and applause.]

The judge gavels again and again shouting for order. "Bailiff, remove every person who persists in disturbing this court!" The courtroom stills.

The judge turns to the attorney for the defense and says, "Counsel, what do you mean by questioning the identity of the accused? He is certainly Mr. Cleaver."

Defense attorney: "Your honor, no offense was intended but, with your permission, I wish to establish certain facts pertaining to my client's true identity. May I proceed?"

The judge grumbles, "Very well. You may proceed."

Defense attorney: "Our entire judicial system is based on the interactions of crime, punishment and rehabilitation. The defendant has, as we have just argued, already been punished through his exile and prison time already served. Further punishment would be neither appropriate nor essential toward the restoration of his usefulness in society.

He is already rehabilitated as we have witnessed through earlier recitals about his life, attitudes and labors since his return from exile.

"And Eldridge Cleaver is truly a different man than the one involved in the Oakland shootout. Even the *Berkeley Barb* thinks so. I would now like to read into the court record the *Barb's* editorial comment: 'The crimes are so old that a different person will be tried for them. . . . Eldridge is going to be tried for a lot of stuff . . . that he would have no more to do with now, than a hole in the head.' "

The attorney for the defense continues, "Massive evidence proves that, beyond a shadow of a doubt, Eldridge Cleaver is now a law-abiding citizen and I might add—a patriot. And so, I petition you, jury of one, in the interest of justice, acquit this man!

"The defense rests."

The judge turns to instruct you, the jury. "If you convict Mr. Cleaver on each of the charges outstanding against him, his prison sentence could range up to 72 years. He could be locked up until 113 years of age. I must in the interest of justice warn you to avoid all emotional feelings for or against the defendant and render your verdict solely on the facts. We now recess the court in order that you, the jury, may closet yourself to deliberate the evidence. Please return when you have arrived at a verdict in the case of—The People Versus Eldridge Cleaver. Jury dismissed."

Now, jury, weigh the evidence and decide his fate. How shall Mr. Cleaver spend the rest of life here on earth?

But even while you are deliberating, Eldridge Cleaver is being tried in still another court. It could be most illuminating to listen in on its proceedings. Most believe that the highest possible level at which a case can be taken is to the Supreme Court or perhaps to the World Court. But, if we are very attentive, we shall soon discover that this court session is taking place at a higher level yet. The place is a Court before which each person will someday appear. We are about to hear the Cleaver case being deliberated in The Court of courts:

JUDGE OF JUDGES: "Advocate, you may now proceed."

THE ADVOCATE: "Eldridge Cleaver, how do you plead?"

ELDRIDGE CLEAVER: "Guilty! I confess that I have violated THE LAW many, many times. I am guilty, but I now ask forgiveness by the Judge of judges and in The Advocate's name ask for a total pardon."

THE ACCUSER: "Judge, long ago you personally warned about such types as the old Cleaver and his former friends, through your prophet Isaiah, who cried, 'Their works are works of iniquity, and an act of violence is in their hands. Their feet run to evil, and they hasten to shed innocent blood; their thoughts are thoughts of iniquity; devastation and destruction are in their highways. They do not know the way of peace, and there is no justice in their tracks; they have made their paths crooked. . . .'

"Cleaver has admitted his guilt and must be consigned for infinity down in Eternal Prison."

THE ADVOCATE: "No, he must not be sent there."

THE ACCUSER: "The Law is binding! You, yourself wrote it, the penalty of violating any of The Law is death. He must be sent down to Eternal Prison. Judge of judges, you must destroy Cleaver!"

THE JUDGE OF JUDGES: "Eldridge Cleaver, I must ask you this question: Do you believe on the previous work and the person of My Son, your Advocate?"

ELDRIDGE CLEAVER: "Yes, I do believe on Him. I first met Him from my balcony in France and I shall never change my mind about your Son."

JUDGE OF JUDGES: "Eldridge Cleaver, so long as you live on earth you will suffer certain consequences for your past violations of The Law: And further, since you will continue making your own choices, your future will be dependent on you alone. Do you understand this, Eldridge Cleaver?"

ELDRIDGE CLEAVER: "Yes, I do, JUDGE OF JUDGES."

THE JUDGE OF JUDGES: "The Law says '... if we freely admit that we have sinned, we find Him reliable and just—He forgives our sins and makes us thoroughly clean from all that is evil';[3] and 'no matter how deep the stain of your sins, I can take it out and make you as clean as freshly fallen snow. Even if you are stained as red as crimson, I can make you white as wool.'[4]

"In view of Eldridge's own testimony, this is My verdict: Because of his personal confession of guilt; because of his petitioning of THE COURT OF COURTS for forgiveness; because of his confession of the work and person of My Son, his ADVOCATE, I hereby grant Eldridge Cleaver an eternal pardon and issue his passport to the Kingdom of Heaven.

"COURT dismissed!"

"There was a time I wouldn't talk to a Christian. But now I have a brand new set of friends and a brand new song to sing."
— Eldridge, 1977[5]

The End

HOW YOU CAN HELP

For many years Eldridge's needs were supplied by his former communist and leftist friends. Upon his return from exile, Mr. Cleaver began to speak out for God and for those things which are worthy about America.

Two large sources of income dried up completely.

(1) His former friends stopped all support to him.

(2) All royalties from his previous books were impounded.

Eldridge Cleaver urgently needs our help. Money is needed to take care of the family living expenses. Even more pressing are some $200,000 in unpaid bills, involving expenses for his legal defense.

I am going to ask you to mail a check to help Eldridge. Please do it today since time is very important. God will mightily bless you for this sacrificial expression of love and of practical help.

Thank you,

George Otis

Make your check to:
ELDRIDGE AND KATHLEEN CLEAVER
P.O. Box 7491
Van Nuys, Calif. 91409

G.M.T. PHOTO

162

APPENDIX I

Optional Reading...

THE "NEW" PANTHERS

"Nothing has changed in the communist ideology. Their goals of global domination are as they were."
— Alexander Solzhenitsyn

Never turn your back on a panther but neither is there reason to fear him when you know his ways. Communist tactics have always been to use the tools of their enemy against him whenever possible. The Panthers' emergence into the political arena is perfectly in line with communist strategy.

Eldridge Cleaver knows their intentions and has warned us.

Four years ago, a Freedom House survey found a third of the world's population—1 1/3 billion people—then lived in what they judged to be free countries. In the short time since then, a 1977 Freedom House report shows that the total has dropped to an alarming 19.6 percent, or one fifth—only 800 million free people left out of the world's 4 billion total!

As much as I'd like to give you a good report on the health of our Black Panther, I can't. It still has the hammer and sickle disease. Perhaps it contracted the disease from a couple of its ferocious animal friends.

Yes, the Bear and the Dragon are each breathing fire, scorching men and nations. Communism's vanguard of agitators, guerrillas and terrorists, is restlessly moving to gobble more territory. The Marxist logic of peace through hatred gained a permanent foothold in the 1917 Russian uprising. Beginning with a mere handful of men, the red cancer has now infected well over one billion of the earth's inhabitants.

All this communist marauding is vividly pictured in the book of Habakkuk: ". . . that fierce and impetuous people who march throughout the earth to seize dwelling places which are not theirs. They are dreaded and feared; their justice and authority originate with themselves. All of them come for violence. Their hoard of faces moves forward. They collect captives like sand." How appropriate! The Bible also previews the end of their haughty leaders: "But they will be held guilty, they *whose strength* is their god." God always has the final word!

The McCarthy Syndrome

Senator Joseph McCarthy died a ridiculed and broken man; hooted to death by the press. They wrote, "The Senator sees a communist under every bed and behind every bush."

In recent decades America became so engrossed in flailing the carcass of Joe McCarthy, it didn't have time to watch Moscow and Peking. Senator McCarthy may turn over in his grave, but it appears he has proved to be of more help to the communists than their stealing of our atom bomb. He was loud-mouthed about the reds at a time America didn't want to be disturbed, when it had its fill of warnings, tension and fighting. But concerning his warnings of dangers from the communists—Joe McCarthy was right.

The problem was: He was right in the wrong way and at the wrong season. The fact is, McCarthyism somehow deadened American senses to the reality of communist infiltration. This enabled the reds to move across the globe with minimal interference from the only country capable of stopping it—the U.S.

What does this have to do with the Black Panther Party?

Plenty, because the Party leans heavily toward the Marxist-Leninist line. Some people thought the Panthers died like the Bull Moose Party. Well, it's very much alive, directed through Chairperson Elaine Brown. A statement issued by the Black Panther Party on April 15, 1976 will help us take the pulse of our cantankerous cat:

"Today the Black Panther Party formally condemns and denounces Eldridge Cleaver as an active and willing agent in the FBI's Cointelpro plan to destroy black organizations by creating internal dissensions. Further, the Black Panther Party formally condemns and denounces Eldridge Cleaver for the murders of Bobby Hutton, the first member and treasurer of the Black Panther Party; Samuel Napier, the circulation and distribution manager of the Black Panther newspaper; and other dedicated Party members who sacrificed their young lives in the cause of freedom and liberation. It is for these acts of blatant and vicious murder—not for the alleged assaults against police—who are, in fact, his conspirators, that the coward Eldridge Cleaver must stand trial by a jury of his peers.

"On the night of April 6, 1968, while emerging from the burning ruins of what had been a family residence at 1218 28th Street in Oakland, the frightened and naked wreckage of what was once a man, Eldridge Cleaver, shoved 17-year-old Bobby Hutton in front of him, intentionally pushing the half-blinded brave black youth into the sights of dozens of police shotguns and rifles, ready to kill without hesitation anything that moved. On April 17, 1971, on Cleaver's orders, agents entered the Black Panther Party's distributing center in New York City with guns drawn to murder Sam Napier. Doing as they were told to do, the agents of Cleaver tied Sam's hands and feet, put cotton in his ears and over his eyes, proceeded to shoot him six times in his head with a .357 magnum and burned his body. There are other Black Panther Party members whose deaths Eldridge Cleaver is responsible for. There are tape-recorded Cleaver threats to assassinate Black Panther Party founder and leader, Huey P. Newton, and Black Party Chairperson, Elaine Brown. There are betrayals and lies. When the Black Panther Party files suit against the FBI, the name of Eldridge Cleaver will be included."[1]

Eldridge, I guess we don't have to ask whether you're a member anymore!

In the November 27, 1976 issue of the Black Panther newspaper, Elaine Brown wrote an article, "Whatever Happened to the Black Panther Party?" In it there are many statements, including a review of the Party's 10-Point manifesto. A few excerpts:

"Many times people say our 10-Point program is reformist, but they ignore the fact that revolution is a process . . . a lot of so-called revolutionaries simply do not understand the statement made by Chairman Mao that 'political power grows out of the barrel of a gun . . .' The emphasis is on the 'grows.' The culmination of political power is the ownership and control of the land and the institutions. . . . But war can only be abolished with war; and in order to get rid of the gun, it is necessary to take up the gun. . . . The gun, by all revolutionary principles, is a tool to be used in our strategy."

We are beginning to hear you, "comrade."

The *Rādix* magazine in 1976 carried, "An Interview With Eldridge Cleaver." In this interview *Rādix* asked: "Have you had any kind of conversation with the Panthers?"

Eldridge Cleaver: "No. Around New Year's Day of this year, I called the Black Panther office to wish them a happy new year. I called collect from the federal prison in San Diego. A man answered the phone, and the operator said, 'I have a collect call from Eldridge Cleaver; will you accept the charges?' The guy laughed and said, 'Wait a minute.' There was about 10 minutes of silence. A couple of times someone came on and said, 'Wait a minute.' Then the guy came back and said, 'We will not accept the call.' I was in jail, but I laughed because it was the phone number of the newspaper I had started; that, part of the Black Panther Party refused to accept a collect call from me; and I was in jail. I thought, 'Well, maybe they're right; but I can't go along with their politics now.' Then I found out that they

168

were part of Ron Dellum's machine in the 8th Congressional District. On top of that I found out that the black judge named Wilson was part of that group and that I had to go before him on my case. And then I found out that John George, who was part of that group, was a candidate for supervisor—and that he had just won the election."

Human Events carried an article, "Dellums and Harrington, Dangerous Choices for CIA Panel." Here are some fascinating excerpts about the Black Panther Party's friend, Congressman Ronald V. Dellums (Democrat, California).

"Dellums ran for and won a seat in the Congress with the coalition support of all leftist, radical and revolutionary elements (Community for New Politics, Panthers, etc.) in his district. . . .

"He gave the clenched fist salute to his supporters at his '70 Congressional election victory rally, telling them his district has just elected a radical. In his first year in the House, he demanded to know why he could not buy *The Black Panther* and *Quicksilver Times* (Washington's revolutionary underground paper) in House restaurants.

"He delivered a bitter, anti-U.S. tirade before the . . . gathering of world communists and U.S. haters in Stockholm, November 28-30, 1970. His speech drew great applause and was reprinted in several foreign languages for worldwide distribution by the sponsoring group (which included leaders of Moscow's major global fronts). . . .

"Dellums has repeatedly and consistently supported professed communist and revolutionary black groups which preach and practice violence and killing to achieve their goals. . . ."

And finally from the *Human Events* article, "He has refused to disavow his support of the Panthers no matter how brazenly they proclaim they are revolutionary communists aiming to destroy the United States, no matter who they have killed—policemen, civilians, blacks, whites, their own members—and no matter how brutal their killing methods."[2]

Yes, the Black Panther is still alive. During a recent interview with a Black Panther Party member from the Bay area, it was revealed that the Party has begun to worm its way into the American political system: doing it by running their own candidates, supporting candidates with similar political views, and registering their people to vote.

He said, "We really don't have any faith in the electoral system; in fact, we have called for the abolition of the office of President."[3]

About the Panther Party working in politics, he commented: "It's also a way—as Elaine (Brown) always says—'to mess with the machinery.' "[4]

This political tinkering must be viewed as a means to an end.

The Panther went on to say "The implementation of the programs and the general strategy of bringing revolution to this country has always been the bottom mark of the Black Panther Party; and we still believe in revolution."[5]

Question: "Are there any Party members in office today?"

Black Panther: "Erica Huggins—in fact, she's the director of the Oakland Community School. She's a member of the Alameda County Board of Education ... and Elaine Brown, of the Board of Commissioners ... well, that controls the policies of education throughout the entire county—1.3 million populace.... We back certain candidates. Ron Dellums, for example, and a brother named Johnny George, who was the first black on the County Board of Supervisors.... There is no such thing as a quiet revolution. We are interested in revolution power."[6]

Panther Chairperson Elaine Brown was sent as a delegate to the 1976 Democratic Convention. She was among those delegates headed by California Governor Jerry Brown, which helped select Carter as the Democrat's Presidential candidate.

How do you like *them* peanuts?

You will be hearing more from the Panther Party as it

works to apply Marxist-Leninist dialectic at every opportunity. Its present activity is a $100 million lawsuit against U.S. law and security agencies.

Remember now, never turn your back on a panther, but neither is there reason to fear him when you know his ways.

Eldridge was right when, after returning from years spent in communist inner sanctums, he warned America it could face another Pearl Harbor. Will it be too late before the U.S. realizes that the communist responds best to the language of power? Mao Tse-Tung immortalized this power-penchant when he established as a communist principle: "Power grows out of the barrel of a gun."

We have seen this concept at work: In Czechoslovakia, where Russian tanks were ordered to crush the "rebels"—freedom-loving Czechs who were resisting—Solzhenitsyn's report of Stalin's monthly massacre of 40,000.

The Vietnam Scab

The American experience in Vietnam was so traumatic! We must learn from the Indochina failure. In spite of an $80 billion annual expenditure for weapons, it still takes a forceful Senate to authorize a trigger to be pulled in the defense of freedoms.

The Russians know this. The Chinese know this. The Cubans know this.

The U.S. was licked in Vietnam by a third-rate power. Why? Largely because America played by the Marquis of Queensbury rules—the communists played to win. The war wasn't lost in Vietnam—it was lost in Washington. We had the tools to win but kept them locked up. The Cambodian victors have since committed genocide on 1 million of their vanquished.

Do you remember how the Vietnam peace talks had been bogged down by Hanoi for years? Richard Watergate finally sent his bombers over Hanoi for a few days.

Fulbright had apoplexy! The doves beat their wings furiously!

But the communists had been spoken to in their own language—power.

The reds quickly rushed back to the peace talk table.

Soon Nixon was invited to Peking—Fulbright and McGovern weren't.

Still we must give credit to the dedicated communist for one of his qualities: perseverance. He is often more dedicated and stubborn in pushing for his cause than most Christians.

He is willing, for years even, to be rebuffed, ridiculed and defeated; he doesn't give up—"two steps forward and one step back" principle. He will give his life and family to advance his atheistic cause. Christians would do well to emulate.

One Party member wrote to a Christian whom he had met during a visit to Moscow: "Believe me, it is we who will win, for we believe in our communist message and we are ready to sacrifice all, even our lives, in order that our cause shall triumph. But you Christians are afraid to soil your hands."[7]

Can the U.S. ever again find the will to use its power in a crisis of justice? Will our defense machine rust for lack of Washington leadership? What would we do if Israel is attacked for the fifth time; and if she's being destroyed?

Yes, Vietnam was the American nightmare! They said it was too far away and not worth helping. Our press said, "President Thieu isn't a nice man. He isn't running a democratic society—not enough freedom of speech and information, you know."

Well, Thieu's gone.

Now, American press, where are those freedoms and where is that flow of information from Vietnam?

I'm sorry, but you are looking stupid.

So the North Vietnamese reneged on the Paris accord. Wasn't it Lenin who declared, "Promises are piecrusts, made to be broken."

Angola was also too far away. That was none of

172

America's business anyhow. Just some "patriots" liberating their country from a repressive government.

Right?

Then what are all those Cuban soldiers doing in there and why that $1 billion in Russian and Chinese tanks, guns and warplanes?

Mourn for the "liberated" Angolans.

Next on the communist agenda: South Africa? The media is talking again: "Those horrible inequalities in Rhodesia and South Africa. Bad people running both countries."

Well, these governments must be severely criticized for their terrible racial irregularities.

But isn't there some way to help our black brothers in Rhodesia and South Africa other than to throw them to the communist alligators?

But, southern Africa is so-o-o far away. America mustn't get involved! Remember Vietnam! Come now, you don't really believe the communists are involved down there. Isn't it just an internal squabble?

The answer is a definite YES. The reds are at it again. Their compassionate, loving hearts are wanting to "liberate" those poor blacks just like they "liberated" the Czechoslovakians.

Surely the reds wouldn't be drooling over the fact that South Africa controls the tanker sea lanes? They aren't ogling the South African gold, diamonds and chromium, are they?

Perish the thought! Everyone knows how much the communists despise wealth.

Excuse me, Kremlin, your slip is showing!

Eldridge Cleaver and Solzhenitsyn are both right. America must shake herself. The ghost of old Joe McCarthy has risen up to haunt us.

McCarthy's ghost is creeping toward our own porch. If Vietnam, Angola and South Africa are too far away, then how about Cuba and maybe Mexico next? How would you like to attempt to secure a 1,800-mile border soon against infiltrating terrorists?

Ask Israel.

You say, "It couldn't happen in America."

Tell 'em, Eldridge.

The new Eldridge

APPENDIX II

By George Otis III
SOUL ON ICE

"The price of hating other human beings is loving oneself less. . . . That is why I started to write. To save myself."[1]

What does one do while spending, on the average, seventeen hours a day in a prison cell? *"For years you have no worries about social life, about girls; you don't even have to take care of your own laundry. You get sharp, you study and learn. You examine yourself."*[2]

With an imposed discipline and the solitude available on the suburbs of society, prison life served to hone the latent communicative talents of one of America's top newsmakers. Maxwell Geismar has heralded Eldridge Cleaver as "simply one of the best cultural critics" in print. To examine this extraordinary man while ignoring his remarkable literary accomplishment would be tantamount to our neglecting to discuss acting in a dialogue with Richard Burton.

During the course of the last decade, Cleaver's bestselling *Soul on Ice* has found rest on bookshelves the world over—from ghetto shoeboxes to spacious university libraries. "A book for which we have to make room," reviewed *The New Republic*, "but not on the shelves we have already built."

It is sometimes difficult to gauge the impact of a work such as *Soul on Ice*. Ofttimes the would-be analyst in his haste to unveil the true state of things leaves his followers adrift in a sea of speculation. For our purposes, however, suffice it to say that any book which has sold millions of copies deserves a closer look.

Reaction to the book has been as widespread and diverse as its audience. Running the gamut of emotional response, *Soul on Ice* has evoked fear, fantasy, anger and, likely, new understanding. Winding and slashing through topics as raw and sensitive as rape and revolution, prison and prejudice, author Eldridge Cleaver, a man described in one review as "no damned gentleman," succeeded in discovering and traumatizing America's central nervous system.

For Cleaver, already well on the road to socialism when he wrote *Soul On Ice,* the real target was the "ofay" power structure—the bigoted, bourgeois, white American system of success through dominance. His basic arguments are, for the most part, concentrated within part II, suggestively entitled *"Blood of the Beast."*

Cleaver begins by describing his defection from Elijah Muhammed (former Black Muslim head) and Muslim terminology in favor of a more sophisticated and distinctive form of socialism. The "white devils" became "imperialists" and "colonialists." But lest we find ourselves too entangled in semantics, Cleaver is quick to remind us of the focal point of all black people. "What we share in common is the desire to break the ofay's power over us."[3] It is somewhat unclear here whether the "us" represents the proletariat or the blacks. Regardless, both needed a champion and Cleaver saw the light.

One of the early tasks at hand was exposing the practice of "Negro control." By inflating the images of various black athletes and entertainers, "The mass media," Cleaver charged, "were able to channel and control the aspirations and goals of the black masses."[4] Thus the problem was removed from the political arena.

There was, however, one major, even pivotal exception. Cleaver's analysis of the Muhammad Ali - Floyd Patterson fight is so remarkable one almost feels the event was viewed from the cockpit of a white man's soul. "The white hope for a Patterson victory was, in essence, a desire to force the Negro, now in rebellion and personified by Ali, back into his 'place'. The black hope, on the contrary, was to see

Uncle Tom defeated, to be given symbolic proof of the victory of autonomous Negro over the subordinate Negro."[5]

"Over many generations," Cleaver wrote, "the black man fell victim of self-contempt."[6] As long as this low self-image was acceptable to blacks no message of aggressive advancement was promulgated. "Slaves," said Frederick Douglas, "are generally expected to sing as well as to work." Cleaver bristled at the thought, "Why is there dancing and singing in the slave quarters?! A slave who dies of natural causes cannot balance two dead flies in the scales of eternity."[7]

Muhammad Ali according to Cleaver was a revolutionary, "the black Fidel Castro of boxing." Ali had usurped the heavyweight crown from "white" America and refused in the process to be manipulated by whites attempting to control his public image. "With the coming of Muhammad Ali, the puppet master was left with a handful of strings to which his dancing doll was no longer attached. A racist Black Muslim heavyweight champion is a bitter pill for racist white America to swallow."[8]

With Muhammed Ali's assistance, use of blacks in the exercise of "Negro control" became increasingly difficult. Be that as it may, there were other problems that were yet in desperate need of attention. The suppression of the Negro for example, according to Cleaver, was nothing short of an internal colonization. "The new left understands this thoroughly. It also knows that America's support of colonialism must be shattered."[9]

It is precisely at this juncture that Cleaver himself falls prey. During the last few decades, particularly amongst the third world nations, millions have risen up in the name of individual liberty to throw off the yoke of bondage. In the process a distinctive revolutionary vocabulary began to dominate their communication. It originated with various revolutionary heroes who, if the truth were known, are themselves indefatigably proficient at administrating repressive regimes while making it a point to personally sample the capitalist life-style. From Brezhnev's collection of foreign sports cars, to Marshal Tito's private planes and castles, to Castro's luxurious Cuban villa they all add up to hypocrisy.

Cleaver went on to say, "The road to the left is the way of reconciliation with the exploited peoples of the world, the liberation of all peoples, the dismantling of all economic relations based upon the exploitation of man by man, universal disarmament. . . . The road to the right is refusal to submit to the universal demand for national liberation, economic justice, peace, and popular sovereignty."[10]

It remains puzzling in light of developments in socialist nations why any individual would give up his freedom in the name of individual liberty, surrendering to the guardianship of a gigantic apparatus of compulsion and coercion, the Socialist state.

Austrian economist Ludwig Von Mises was equally incredulous when he wrote, "They call themselves Democrats, but they yearn for dictatorship. They call themselves revolutionaries, but they want to make the government omnipotent. They promise the blessings of the Garden of Eden, but they plan to transform the world into a gigantic post office. Every man but one a subordinate clerk in a bureau, what an alluring utopia! What a noble cause to fight for!"[11]

By the early 1950s it was evident that Stalinist Russia was a "god that failed." During the tense years of the cold war against this brutal, totalitarian state there were few if any anti-American protests at home or abroad. It seemed to be a relatively equal standoff with two titans threatening and glaring at the other.

With the advent of the Vietnam conflict, however, cries of "imperialism" began to echo throughout the land. Here was a totally different situation from the cold war. Here was the powerful yankee bully brandishing his might against the poor defenseless Vietcong in their rice paddies. The Vietnam war was an opportunity that liberals, militants and leftists had long awaited. Cleaver was not to miss his chance, either, to denounce the "imperialist aggressor" for "unleashing its anxious fury"[12] against the Orientals in Southeast Asia. But Cleaver was more interested in the black man's stake in Vietnam. He cried out for blacks to organize their trojan horse "to change the foreign and domestic policies of the U.S. government."[13] As he saw it, the American government had a double purpose in sending balck troops to Vietnam. First to kill off the cream of black youth and secondly to spread hatred for the black race throughout Asia.

Cleaver in a rather amusing fashion denounced the "lewd spectacle of dixiecratic dinosaurs."[14] He decried the actions of the anti-war protestors from their offices nestled in what Eldridge often referred to as "that omnipotent area," Washington D.C.

Yet we must require of Cleaver, the new left and company, that *they* produce a set of moral guidelines based on principles more stable than their slippery relativism.

There are grave limitations with any position that denies the existence of God and absolutes as its starting premise. John Hallowell of Duke University asked, "how can you condemn a tyrant as unjust when you have purged the word justice from your vocabulary? How, indeed, can you recognize tyranny?"

Liberalism had paved the way for the new left, including the Panthers. With its cult of the suspended judgment, tolerant liberalism became flabby and confused; it had too long allowed itself to be seduced, even raped, by totalitarian ideologies. In its relativistic, bend-over-backward, pragmatic way, it was undermining a civilization in which it no longer believed.

With a system based on relativity through a denial of absolutes, it won't be long before, as John Hallowell so aptly puts it, you will find "despair disguised as humility and indifference parading as tolerance."

We have further to note that the weakening and dissolution of such ties as private property, family and church have not, as many had hoped, liberated men. Instead, they have produced alienation, isolation, and spiritual desolation.

Cleaver felt that largely as a result of unemployment, hatred for the system of private property was steadily mounting within the black community. (That, according to evidence, does seem to be the case.) His ideal, however, of a socialist state, including the automatic abolition of private property, should be viewed in conjunction with the plight of eastern European masses desperately attempting to regain lost freedoms.

It has been estimated that 10 percent of society watches things happen, 10 percent makes things happen and 80 percent doesn't know what's happening!

Well, Mr. Cleaver doesn't possess the constitution to sit idle while history passes him by, nor is he ignorant of geopolitical or socioeconomic developments. Eldridge Cleaver tried and succeeded in his personal attempt to dent history with his formidably analytical mind and as a result, for good or ill, *Soul on Ice,* has become a literary legend in our day.

COMMUNIST GLOSSARY

BOURGEOISIE —

Although the term originally meant "the inhabitants of cities" it was used by Karl Marx to denote all the groups that we now call "white collar workers." Marx often gave a narrow economic definition of the word "those who own the means of production."

PROLETARIAT —

The working class. Those who sell their labor in order to

live. The great mass of common people subject to the Bourgeoisie.

IMPERIALISM — The practice of extending the domain of one nation over another through direct conflict or through indirect control of political and economic circumstances.

COLONIALISM — Basically synonymous with Imperialism. Rulership over cities and countries beyond your own borders.

DIALECTIC — The term originated with the German philosopher Hegel. Basically it is philosophy of change through conflict. Hegel taught that struggle between a particular theory and its opposite produced a completely new product which he termed "synthesis." This struggle was elaborated on by Karl Marx. He pitted the Bourgeoisie against the Proletariat. This conflict, he believed, would in time result in the synthesis of Communism.

THE NEW LEFT — The Old Left represented strict Marxist - Leninist ideas worked out in Soviet Russia. The problem arose when the Proletariat in other European nations, instead of overthrowing the Bourgeoisie, joined the Bourgeoisie. Radicals abroad then formed what they called the New Left. This group included groups such as the SDS, the Weather Underground, and the Yippies. They were prepared to take up the fight where the Old Left had failed.

GUERRILLA —

One who practices an irregular form of hit-and-run warfare. The person who practices guerrilla warfare is usually fighting against an enemy with superior forces and often has returned to his own country to overturn its existing government.

CENTRAL COMMITTEE —

The governing body of the Communist party. The committee includes top-ranking Party members. The Central Committee is turn in governed by a 15-member Presidium or Politburo.

FOOTNOTES

Chapter One

1. *Seize the Time*
2. *The Black Panther*

Chapter Three

1. Wendell Wade Transcripts People's Exhibit No. 67, subsequently repudiated.
2. Terry Cotton Transcripts
3. Oakland Tribune/S.F. Chronicle

Chapter Four

1. *The Black Panther*
2. *Seize the Time*
3. *Seize the Time*

Chapter Five

1. *Eldridge Cleaver: Post Prison Writings*
2. Motion to Dismiss Indictments (Transcripts)

Chapter Eight

1. *I Was a Black Panther*
2. *I Was a Black Panther*
3. *The Black Panther* newspaper
4. *Seize the Time*
5. *Seize the Time*
6. *Seize the Time*
7. *The Black Panthers Speak*
8. *The Black Panthers Speak*

9. *Seize the Time*
10. *Eldridge Cleaver: Post Prison Writings*
11. *Eldridge Cleaver: Post Prison Writings*
12. *Eldridge Cleaver: Post Prison Writings*
13. *Seize the Time*
14. David Hilliard Transcripts
15. *I Was a Black Panther*
16. *I Was a Black Panther*

Chapter Ten

1. The Panther leader in exile wrote this letter to black soldiers
2. *Conversation with Eldridge Cleaver* (Algiers)
3. *Conversation with Eldridge Cleaver* (Algiers)

Chapter Eleven

1. Excerpted from *Ramparts*
2. *The Vanguard*
3. *High Adventure* Television

Chapter Twelve

1. *Soul on Ice*
2. *Soul on Ice*
3. *Soul on Ice*
4. *Soul on Ice*
5. *Soul on Ice*
6. *Soul on Ice*
7. *Soul on Ice*
8. *Soul on Ice*
9. *Soul on Ice*
10. *Soul on Ice*
11. *Soul on Ice*
12. *Soul on Ice*
13. *Soul on Ice*
14. *Soul on Ice*

15. *Soul on Ice*
16. *Soul on Ice*
17. *Soul on Ice*

Chapter Thirteen

1. *Conversation with Eldridge Cleaver* (Algiers)
2. *Soul on Ice*
3. *Soul on Ice*
4. *Eldridge Cleaver: Post Prison Writings*
5. *Soul on Ice*
6. *Soul on Ice*
7. *Soul on Ice*
8. *Soul on Ice*
9. *Eldridge Cleaver: Post Prison Writings*
10. *Soul on Ice*
11. *Soul on Ice*
12. *Soul on Ice*
13. *Soul on Ice*
14. *Conversation with Eldridge Cleaver* (Algiers)
15. *Conversation with Eldridge Cleaver* (Algiers)
16. *Soul on Ice*
17. *Soul on Ice*
18. *The Readers Digest*
19. *Charlotte Observer*
20. NBC's *Meet the Press*
21. *The Readers Digest*
22. *The Readers Digest*
23. *The Readers Digest*
24. *The Readers Digest*
25. *People* magazine
26. *Los Angeles Herald Examiner*
27. *People* magazine
28. *The Readers Digest*
29. NBC's *Meet the Press*
30. Eldridge Cleaver Defense Committee Publication

Chapter Fifteen

1. Soul on Ice
2. Soul on Ice
3. San Diego Church News
4. *through* 19. Excerpts from a composite of interviews and speeches, including TV appearances on *High Adventure,* the *700 Club, PTL, Hour of Power;* also from church messages.

Chapter Sixteen

1. *Los Angeles Times*
2. *Sacramento Bee*

Chapter Seventeen

1. *People* magazine
2. Wm. F. Buckley
3. *New York Times*
4. *New York Times*

Chapter Eighteen

1. *Radix*
2. *Los Angeles Times*
3. 1 John 1:9, *The Living Bible*
4. Isaiah 1:18, *The Living Bible*
5. *Los Angeles Herald Examiner*

Appendix I

1. *Radix*
2. *Human Events*
3. *Human Events*
4. *Human Events*
5. *Human Events*
6. *The Black Panther* newspaper

7. *Friends in the West*

Appendix II

1. *Soul on Ice*
2. *New York Times*
3. *Soul on Ice*
4. *Soul on Ice*
5. *Soul on Ice*
6. *New York Times*
7. *Soul on Ice*
8. *Soul on Ice*
9. *Soul on Ice*
10. *Soul on Ice*
11. *The Conservative Intellectual Movement in America since 1945*
12. *Soul on Ice*
13. *Soul on Ice*
14. *Soul on Ice*

BIBLIOGRAPHY AND RESEARCH RESOURCES

BOOKS

The Black Almanac (Hornsby), Barron's Educational Series, Inc.
I Was a Black Panther (Moore), Doubleday
Black Awakening in Capitalist America (Allen), Doubleday
Do It! (Rubin), Simon and Schuster
The Black Panthers (Marine), Ramparts
Conversation with Eldridge Cleaver (Lockwood), Dell
Soul on Ice (Cleaver), Dell
Seize the Time (Seale), Random House
The Vanguard (Baruch), Beacon Press
Eldridge Cleaver: Post Prison Writings & Speeches (Scheer), Random House
Crisis America (Otis), Bible Voice/Revell
The Black Panthers Speak (Foner), Lippincott
The Writings of Huey P. Newton, Random House

NEWSPAPERS

Radix
Oakland Tribune Sun
San Francisco Chronicle
New York Times
The Black Panther
Berkeley Barb
National Courier
The Charlotte Observer (article by Columnist William Buckley)
Sacramento Bee
Los Angeles Times
San Diego Church News
Human Events

MAGAZINES

The Reader's Digest
Ramparts
People
Prison Evangelism

INTERVIEWS & LECTURES

NBC's *Meet the Press*
High Adventure TV Series
Hour of Power TV
Lectures, TV, radio—varied
Various Interviews with Knowledgeable Sources
Miscellaneous court & police files and transcripts

SCRIPTURE SOURCES

King James Version
American Standard Version
The New American Standard Bible
The Living Bible

ABOUT THE AUTHOR

Author George Otis, former Lear executive, is a man in motion! A 250,000 mile-a-year speaker, host of the *High Adventure* TV series and author of seven books (2 million in print). Otis, his wife Virginia, and their four children call California, and the former James Cagney residence, home. Pat Boone once said of him, "Where does he find the energy? I think he's a guy with one finger stuck in a light socket—the electric man!"

George Otis somehow finds himself in the presence of the extraordinary: stars, champions, kings, achievers, prime ministers, and other assorted mortals. His books have ranged widely; from the role as a futurist in *Millennium Man* to politics in *Crisis America* and *The Blueprint*. Otis's other books include *High Adventure; Peace, Power and Happiness; God, Money and You* and *The Ghost of Hagar.*

The author wants to make clear that this book has been written with neither the authorization nor assistance of Mr. Cleaver. If you should like a gift copy of the entire transcript of Eldridge Cleaver's personal testimony given during that first meeting at Hollywood Assembly, write to High Adventure Ministries, Box 7466, Van Nuys, Calif.

91409. It will be appreciated if you will enclose a check made out to *Eldridge Cleaver* for use toward his urgently needed legal defense costs.

— The Publisher